Snorkel Hawai'i

The Big Island

Guide to the Beaches and Snorkeling of Hawai'i • Judy & Mel Malinowski

Snorkel Hawai'i The Big Island
Guide to the Beaches and Snorkeling of Hawaii

Third Edition © 2008 by Judy and Mel Malinowski

Published by: Indigo Publications
e-mail: indigo@snorkelguides.com
SAN 298-9921
Publisher's symbol: Indigo CA

Printed in China by C & C Offset Printing Co., Inc.

All landscape photography ©Mel Malinowski.
All underwater photography ©Jay Torborg unless otherwise noted.
Other photos courtesy of Ray Lyons and NOAA.

Award-winning photographer Jay Torborg has been photographing nature for almost 30 years. Jay started out focusing on landscape photography, but over the last several years, his photographic interests have shifted toward wildlife and underwater photography. More of Jay's photography can be seen and purchased on his web site: www.torborgphoto.com.

Jay uses Nikon D1X professional digital SLRs with a wide range of professional Nikon lenses for most of his photography. For underwater photography, he uses this same camera mounted in a Seacam housing with two Ikelite 200 strobes.

About the cover: Eyestripe surgeonfish photo by Jay Torborg.

Thanks to the many kind-spirited people of Hawai'i who bring the spirit of aloha to all they do. Special thanks to Dr. John Randall and John Hoover for their helpful counsel, as well as their inspirational and detail-rich reference books on the sea life of our islands. Mahalo to Danny Akaka for advising and teaching us by his example. Through him, we have come to better understand the beauty and value of Hawai'ian language and culture.

ISBN 9780964668096
Library of Congress Control Number: 2008900161

Contents

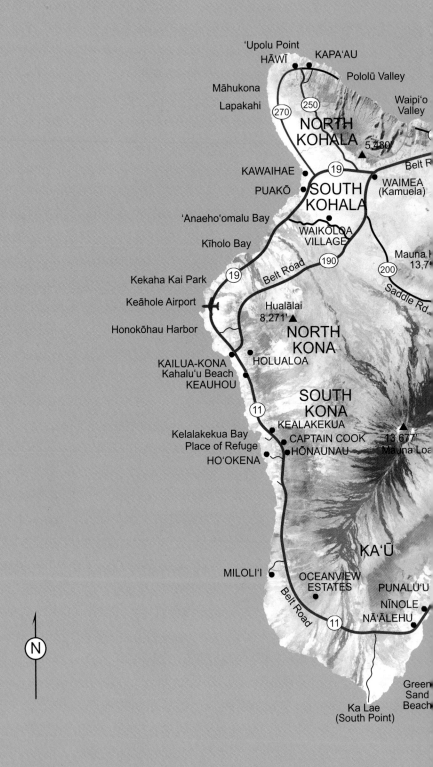

'Upolu Point
HĀWĪ   KAPA'AU
                        Pololū Valley
Māhukona
Lapakahi   Waipi'o
                                      Valley
         270   250
              NORTH
              KOHALA 5,480'

                                      Belt R
KAWAIHAE   19
PUAKŌ   SOUTH   WAIMEA
           KOHALA   (Kamuela)

'Anaeho'omalu Bay
                WAIKOLOA
                VILLAGE
Kīholo Bay

                                 Mauna
                          190   13,7
Kekaha Kai Park   19   200
              Belt Road   Saddle Rd.
Keāhole Airport
                 Hualālai
                 8,271'▲
Honokōhau Harbor
                 NORTH
                 KONA
KAILUA-KONA   HOLUALOA
Kahalu'u Beach
KEAUHOU
                 SOUTH
                 KONA
              11
              KEALAKEKUA
Kelalakekua Bay CAPTAIN COOK 13,677'
Place of Refuge HŌNAUNAU   Mauna Loa
HO'OKENA

                          KA'Ū

MILOLI'I   OCEANVIEW
              ESTATES   PUNALU'U
                          NĪNOLE
              Belt Road   NĀ'ĀLEHU
                       11
                              Green
                              Sand
                              Beach
         Ka Lae
         (South Point)

N

4

Hawai'i Road Map

(Also see Snorkeling Site
Index Map on page 38)

HONOKA'A

HĀMĀKUA

⑲

Laupāhoehoe Point

NORTH
HILO

HONOMŪ

Belt Road

Hilo Bay

Hilo Airport

⑳⓪ SOUTH
HILO

HILO

KEA'AU

Cape Kumukahi

⑪ ⑬⓪

MOUNTAIN
VIEW

Lava
Tree

KAPOHO
Kapoho Tidepools

PĀHOA

POHO'IKI

VOLCANO

PUNA

Hawai'i
Volcanoes
National Park

'93 lava flow

⑬⑦

Kīlauea

KEHENA

Ka'ū
Desert

Belt Road

Chain of Craters Rd.

10   20   30
Kilometers

10   20   30
Miles

Why Snorkel the Big Island?

We came from the sea. Our blood is salty, as are our tears. Many years have passed since our primitive ancestors left the sea, yet the water still beckons in our dreams. Snorkeling allows us to follow those dreams and enjoy the most colorful show on earth.

When you don that mask and snorkel, and gently place your face toward the sea, you've entered another planet—one completely unlike home. Everything works differently here in the sea. It's graceful, soft and inviting, with a dazzling array of color and whimsical life forms. Scuba, with its elaborate, expensive equipment, is one way to enter this world. Snorkeling is a lighter, easier way, a family sport, available to all ages and abilities. Once you've arrived in Hawai'i, it's a remarkable bargain—the best in the islands.

The Big Island offers some of the clearest water and finest sites in all the Hawai'ian islands. Less developed than Maui and O'ahu, it retains much of the aloha spirit. Most kama'aina are friendly, relaxed and willing to share their love of this remarkable island.

Snorkel Hawai'i makes it easy

We've done extensive research that will help you quickly locate appropriate sites to fit your interests and abilities, saving your valuable vacation hours.

Snorkeling sites in Hawai'i are sometimes tricky because of changeable waves and currents, so it's best to get good advice before heading out. Everyone has had their share of unpleasant experiences due to vague directions as well as outdated or inaccurate information. We have created the Snorkel Hawai'i series as that savvy snorkeling buddy everyone needs. We've included many personal stories; see About the Authors on page 224 if you want to know a little more about us.

We live on the Big Island and have snorkeled all the major sites many times. The challenge lies in finding them quickly, knowing how to enter and exit, and deciding where to snorkel, so you'll have a safe and rewarding experience. Our detailed maps and instructions will guide you to all the best snorkeling, saving you time and effort.

Try to visit the island of Hawai'i at least once in your life and by all means experience the underwater world. Aloha!

— Judy and Mel Malinowski

Snorkeling is...

- easy

- relaxing

- fun

- floating on the surface of the sea

- breathing without effort through a tube

- peering into the water world through a mask

- open to any age, size, shape or ability

Who was the first snorkeler? As the fossil records include few petrified snorkels, we are free to speculate.

Among larger creatures, elephants are the pioneers and current champions, as they have known how to snorkel for countless generations. Once in a blue moon, you may see a elephant herd heading out to do lunch on an island off the coast of Tanzania, paddling along with their trunks held high. No one knows whether the hefty pachyderms enjoy the fish-watching, but you can bet a big liquid chuckle reverberates through the ranks of reef fish in the vicinity as the parade goes by.

As evolution continued, perhaps a clever member of the promising Homo sapiens species saved his furry brow by hiding underwater from pursuers, breathing through a hollow reed. Masks came much later, so the fish probably looked a little fuzzy. Surviving to propagate his brainy kind, he founded a dynasty of snorkelers. Perhaps he actually liked the peaceful atmosphere down there, and a new sport was born.

Some of our readers may grumble that snorkeling is not a real sport: no rules, no score, no competition, scarcely aerobic, with hardly any equipment or clothing. We say to them: lighten up, you're on vacation!! Relax in the water—go for a long run later.

Incorrigible competitors can create their own competition by counting how many species they've seen or trying to spot the biggest or the most seen in one day. Everybody else can ease into the welcoming waters of Hawai'i and just have fun being a part of nature's colorful, salty, wet, ancient home.

Basics

To snorkel you need only two things:

Snorkel	Saves lifting your head once a minute, wasting energy and disturbing the fish.
Mask	While you can see (poorly) without one, it keeps the water out of your eyes and lets you see clearly.

Rent them inexpensively at many local shops or buy them if you prefer. It's all the back-to-basics folks need to snorkel in calm warm water, where there aren't any currents or hazards.

Savvy snorkelers often add a few items to the list, based on years of experience, such as:

Swimsuit	Required by law in many localities. Added benefit: saves you from an occasional all-body sunburn.
Fins	Good if you want to swim with ease and speed like a fish. Saves energy. A must in Hawai'i, due to occasional strong currents. They protect your tender feet too.
T-shirt	Simple way to avoid or minimize sunburn on your back. Available everywhere in many colors.
Sunscreen	Save sunscreen for after your snorkel to avoid getting it into your eyes and polluting the reef area. Use a lycra skin instead.
Lycra Skin	A great all-body cover-up for warm weather. Provides much better protection than a T-shirt, and saves gallons of sunscreen. Keeps you from leaving a sunscreen oil slick in your wake. Available in most dive shops, and a good investment.
Wetsuit	For some, the Hawai'ian waters seem a bit chilly, not exactly pool-warm. Wetsuits range from simple T-shirt-like tops to full suits. Worth considering. Fringe benefit: sun protection!

You're almost ready to get wet. But wait! You want to know even more technical detail? Every sport has an equipment list—it's what keeps sporting goods stores in business and your garage shelves full.

8

Gear Selection

Good snorkeling gear enables you to pay attention to the fish instead of uncomfortable distractions. Poor equipment will make you suffer in little ways, from pressure headaches caused by a too-tight mask, to blisters on your feet from ill-fitting fins. Consider your alternatives carefully before buying and you'll have more fun later. This is a case of "pain, no gain." If it hurts, fix it, and you'll be glad you did. You may want to rent & try gear first. See page 145 for tips about renting.

Snorkel

Snorkels can be quite cheap. Be prepared to pony up $25 or more, however, if you want them to last longer and be more comfortable. You'll appreciate a comfortable mouthpiece if you plan to snorkel for long. Watch out for hard edges—a good mouthpiece is smooth and chewy-soft. Some of the more expensive mouthpieces swivel for comfort. We like that better than corrugated models.

Several new high-tech models have been designed to minimize water coming down the tube from chop or an occasional swell overtopping you. We looked at these with mild skepticism until a choppy snorkeling trip had us coughing and clearing our snorkels every third breath. With our new dry snorkels, that water never makes it to the mouthpiece.

Technology continues to advance, so you can now get a snorkel that will keep ALL of the water out, even if you dive beneath the surface. Don't ask us how they do it, but it works well! Even in very choppy conditions, you never worry about water coming in. We like dry snorkels, at about $40 and up. They certainly make learning to snorkel as easy as possible, although they're not a necessity.

These fancier snorkels do need care because you won't want a valve to fail just as you arrive at that perfect destination. Keep them out of the sand! Repairs or replacements are available at most dive shops.

Snorkel Holder

This little guy holds your snorkel to your mask strap, so you don't keep dipping it in the sea. The old standard is a simple figure 8 double loop that pulls over the snorkel tube, wraps around your mask strap, and then back over the tube. A hefty rubber band will work passably in a pinch. The downside of this type of snorkel holder is that it doesn't slide up and down easily, and often gets tangled with long hair. The good news is that there is a better way available. The higher end snorkels often have a slot or movable ring that allows the snorkel to be adjusted easily. It slides easily rather than having to be tugged. The standard scuba snorkel position is on your left side. You might as well get used to it there since you may dive eventually.

Mask

Nothing can color your snorkeling experience more than an ill-fitting mask (unless, of course, you get that all-body sunburn mentioned earlier). Don't settle for painful or leaky masks! If it hurts, it's not your problem—it's the mask that's wrong for you. Remember our snorkeling principle: "pain, no gain"!

Simple variety store masks can cost as little as $10. Top-quality masks from a dive shop run upwards of $60. Consider starting out with a rental mask, paying a bit extra for the better quality models. As you gain more experience, you'll be in a better position to evaluate a mask before you lock yourself into one style.

You need a good fit to your particular facial geometry. Shops often tell you to place the mask on your face (without the strap) and breathe in. If the mask will stay in place, then they say you have found a good fit. However, nearly all masks will stay on my face under this test, yet some leak later! You can do better.

Look for soft edges and a mask that conforms to your face even before drawing in your breath. There's a great deal of variance in where a mask rests on your face and how soft it feels, so compare very carefully. Look for soft and comfortable, unless you especially like having pressure headaches and don't mind looking like a very large octopus glommed on to your face.

Lack of 20-20 vision needn't cut into your viewing pleasure, but it does require a little more effort during equipment selection. Those who wear contact lenses can use them within their masks, taking on the risk that they'll swish out and float softly and invisibly down to the sea bed, perhaps to be found by a fossil hunter in the distant future, but certainly not by you. Use the disposable kind. Unless you use contacts, search for a correctable mask. Vision-correcting lens are available for many masks in 1/2 diopter increments.

If the mask you prefer doesn't offer standard correcting lenses, custom prescription lenses can be fitted to almost any mask. This

Moorish idol

costs more and takes longer. Even bifocals are available. We happen to prefer the comfortable prescription masks made by SeaVision which can be ordered with any custom correction. The cost is much like normal prescription lenses.

Mustaches create a mask leakage problem. As Mel likes the look of a mustache, he has coped with this his entire adult life. Some advise the use petroleum jelly or silicon compound to make a more effective seal. That doesn't appeal to him since he goes in and out of the water several times a day. It does help to choose a mask that rests high over the mouth and perhaps trim the top 1/8 inch or so off the center mustache, if it sticks up. Hair breaks the seal and allows water to seep into the mask slowly, so you'll still have to clear the mask occasionally. Mel tolerated half an inch of water in the bottom of his mask for years, until he got a good purge valve mask. Much better!

His Sea Vision mask mounts a purge valve in the bottom of the nosepiece. If some water leaks in, he just lightly blows a little air out the nose, taking the water with it. This is much easier and more effective than lifting the bottom of the mask to blow the water out.

The conventional wisdom in scuba is that purge valves are an unnecessary weak point. So far, we haven't had any trouble with ours. Some experienced divers do use them and swear by them. This isn't an issue snorkelers need worry about. If you find a purge valve mask that fits well, use it for snorkeling. You'll be glad you did!

Mask Strap

The rubber strap that comes with the mask can tangle your hair. If you have your own mask and want it to slide on more easily, there's a comfortable strap available with velcro adjustment. The back is made of wetsuit material—stretchy and soft. Cost is about $10-15 in dive shops. Since we get in and out often, we happen to prefer this one, but it's a convenience for the frequent snorkeler rather than a necessity and it doesn't dry fast.

Fins

The simplest fins are basic (usually black) enclosed foot fins. These are one-piece molded rubber and slip right on to your bare feet. For basic snorkeling, these inexpensive fins are fine. We own several kinds of fins and still sometimes choose the one-piece foot fins for lightness and compact packing. They seem to last forever and are inexpensive ($15-$25). Mel has had to shave off the sharp edge just under where your toes go, as it sticks up too far and rubs. This is easy to do with a carpet knife.

Why should anyone look further? Because it is possible to get better comfort and more thrust. Specialized fins are now made for higher performance and can run $100 or more.

Long stiff fins are excellent for surface diving and speed, but can be tiring and cause muscle cramps if you're not an athlete.

Scuba divers often use strap-on fins with wetsuit booties. They're available in lots of colors and styles, but float your feet too high for efficient snorkeling. Soft, split blade fins are our current favorites because they are comfortable and less tiring when snorkeling long distance or through rough water. Oceanic Vortex are particularly comfortable if you have a narrow foot. While they may seem too soft for speed, we find them excellent for hours of snorkeling.

If you're inclined to get blisters, pay more attention to softness and fit. Liners are available, but usually not necessary. Blisters are NOT inevitable, so some people may need to keep hunting for the best fins for the shape of untypical feet. Unless it's absolutely certain that no current can carry you away,

ALWAYS WEAR FINS!

As you look at more advanced fins, they split into two attachment methods with pros and cons to each type. We own both and pick the best for a particular situation.

ENCLOSED FOOT	Your bare foot slides into a stretchy, integral molded rubber shoe.
Advantages	The lightest, most streamlined and fish-like fit. It probably is the most efficient at transmitting your muscle power to the blade. We prefer this type when booties are not required for warmth or safety. We find that we almost always choose and wear this kind.
Disadvantages	The fins must be closely fitted to your particular foot size and shape. Some models may cause blisters. You need to find a brand that fits the shape of your foot well. If you have to hike in to the entry site, you need separate shoes. This may preclude entering at one spot, and exiting elsewhere. If the entry is over sharp coral or other hazards, these may not be the best choice. But you really shouldn't be walking on the coral anyway.
STRAP-ON	Made for use with booties.
Advantages	Makes rough surface entry easy. Just hike to the entry point, head on into the water holding your fins in hand, and lay back to pull on your fins. Exiting is just as easy. The bootie cushions your foot, making blisters unlikely. Widely used for scuba.
Disadvantages	Less streamlined. The bootie makes your feet float up, so you may have trouble keeping your fins from breaking the surface.

No matter how good the fins, snorkeling for long hours may cause blisters—especially on the heel. No need to worry if you carry 3M Nexcare waterproof bandages. These little essentials will do the job and stay in place well when wet. Buy them at any major pharmacy.

Reef Shoes or Booties

Walking with bare feet on 'a'a (sharp lava) or coral can shred your feet in a quick minute. There are fine reef shoes available that are happy in or out of the water. These are primarily for getting there, or wading around, as they don't really work that well with strap-on fins.

For the sake of the reef, don't actually walk on a reef with reef shoes, since each step kills hundreds of the little animals that make up the living reef.

Zip-on booties are widely used by divers and allow use of strap-on fins. They do float your feet—a disadvantage for snorkelers.

Keeping Time

One easy-to-forget item: a water-resistant watch. This needn't be expensive and is very useful for pacing yourself and keeping track of your sun exposure time.

"Water resistant" alone usually means that a little rain won't wreck the watch, but immersion in water may. When a designation like "to 10 meters" is added, it denotes added water-resistance; but the dynamic pressures from swimming increase the pressure, so choose 50 meters or greater rating to be safe even when snorkeling. Don't take a 50 meter watch scuba diving, though—that requires 100-200 meter models.

Hawai'ian time is two hours earlier than Pacific Standard Time (winter) or three hours earlier than Pacific Daylight Time. Hawai'i doesn't observe Daylight Savings Time.

Body Suit

There are a variety of all-body suits that protect you from sun exposure and light abrasion, but provide no warmth. They are made from various synthetic fabrics—lycra and nylon being common. They cost much less than wetsuits and are light and easy to pack.

We usually bring ours along as a sun protection alternative in warmer conditions. If you don't want to look like a F.O.B. (Fresh Off the Boat) tourist, with a shocking pink outline of your swimsuit, plan ahead about sun protection. You'll sleep better if you do. The coral and fish will not miss all that sunscreen fouling their water. And you'll be able to snorkel longer, in the middle of the day if you want, without the risk of that trip-ruining painful sunburn.

Wetsuit

In Hawai'i, water temperature on the surface varies from a low of about 75° F in March to a high of about 80° F in September. If you happen to be slender, no longer young or from a moderate climate, this can seem cold. Sheltered bays and tidepools can be a bit warmer while deeper water can be surprisingly cold. Fresh water runoff can also make water cooler than you might expect. We've snorkeled in March when we swore it was not a bit warmer than 65° off Kaua'i. Maybe not, but even two degrees cooler feels like six or eight!

Regardless of the exact temperature, the water is cooler than your body. With normal exertion, your body still cools bit by bit. After awhile, perhaps 30-45 minutes, you start feeling a little chilly. Later you begin shivering and eventually hypothermia begins.

We often snorkel for more than an hour. A thin, 3mm full wetsuit protects us from the sun while keeping us warm and comfortable in the summer and fall. Some folks don't need this in warmer weather. Others like us have little natural padding, get cold easily. In the cooler winter and spring water, we either add a "core warmer" on top of our 3mm suits, or switch to a 5mm full wetsuit.

Off the rack suits are a bargain and fit most folks. Look for a snug fit at neck, wrists and ankles—if your suit is loose there, water will flow in and out, making you cold. If you have big feet and small ankles, get zippers on the legs if possible or you'll really have to struggle to remove the suit when it's wet.

Wetsuit wearers also get added range and buoyancy, and they hardly need a life jacket! Wearing a wetsuit, you can stay in the water without hypothermia for many hours—even in the winter. This could be comforting in the unlikely event that some strong current sweeps you off towards Fiji. There are few situations from which you can't rescue yourself if you're wearing a wetsuit and fins.

We've found a wetsuit favorite brand, Henderson Wetsuits from New Jersey. We like their variety of wetsuits for different purposes. Our favorite model is called "Hyperstretch Titanium", because the superstretchability of the fabric makes it easy to get on and off, it adapts to various body shapes, and flexes with you as you swim. It is unquestionably the most comfortable wetsuit we own. However, we have noticed that it is not quite as warm for a given thickness as some of their other models. The three millimeter-thick version is light, and warm enough for Hawai'i summer and fall snorkeling. Thicker versions that are warmer are also available. Other types include Gold Core (easier to slide on and off) and Instadry, which scarcely absorbs water. Instadry is stiffer and stickier than the other models, but it has an important advantage: you can shake the water off it, and little water is left. This is great for repetitive snorkeling from a boat, or travel. It has become our travel favorite.

Henderson has been promoting layered systems. The idea is to wear a thin full wetsuit, and then add a core warmer on top, which is like a shorty, but without sleeves. We've come around to liking this system, as it allows you to easily adjust the warmth to the conditions.

Dave Barry once described putting on a wetsuit as like wrestling with an octopus. Not this one! No more hanging onto the shower while your buddy tries to pull the wetsuit off your ankles with a winch. If you can afford the extra cost, these suits are superb. We had ours custom-made with longer arms and legs, and no rubberized kneepads. We like our wetsuits sleek and flexible, and we never wear out the knees.

Swim Cap

If you have trouble with long hair tangling in your mask straps while snorkeling, get a lycra Speedo swim cap. It may look silly, but it works, and also protects your scalp from too many rays.

Snorkeling Vest

It is possible to buy inflatable vests made for snorkeling. Some guidebooks and stores promote them as virtually essential. We've taken excursions that require all snorkelers to wear one. Other excursions encourage the use of flotation noodles or kick boards—whatever it takes to make you comfortable.

Vests are hardly necessary in salt water for most people, but can be useful if you can't swim a lick or won't be willing to try this sport without it. There is a possible safety edge for kids or older folks. If you do get a vest, you can give it to another beginner after you get used to snorkeling. You will discover that it takes little effort to float flat in salt water while breathing through a snorkel.

If you feel you need extra flotation, consider using a light wetsuit instead of a life vest. It simultaneously gives you buoyancy, sun and critter protection, as well as warmth.

Low Volume Masks

When you begin looking at masks, the variety can be bewildering. How can you figure out which design is best for you?

Inexpensive masks often have one large flat front glass. They're OK if the skirt of the mask fits you, although they're often a bit stiff and uncomfortable. They also tend to be far out from your face with a big air space. As you go up in price, the lenses tend to get smaller and closer to your eyes, as preferred by divers.

There is a good scuba reason for this. These are called low volume masks. They contain less airspace and so require less effort to clear when water gets in. They also press less against your face when you go deeper and the pressure rises (if you forget to blow higher pressure air in through your nose) and hence are more comfortable when diving.

For a snorkeler this is of little importance, but it still should be considered as you select your mask. Many snorkelers go on to do some surface diving, as well as Snuba or scuba diving. When you dive down even 10 feet, the water pressure is considerable. At 32 feet, the air in your lungs and mask is compressed to half its volume. Unless you blow some air into your mask through your nose, the pressure on your face can be quite uncomfortable!

If your mask is flooded, which does happen, it is easier to clear out a low volume mask. So, while it's not the most important factor, if everything else is equal, low volume is better.

Surface Diving Gear

For surface diving, bigger fins improve your range. Those surreal-looking Cressi fins that seem about three feet long will take you down so fast you'll be amazed. You'll also be amazed how few suitcases are big enough to accommodate them, and how inadequate your legs feel to kick them for an hour, unless you're very athletic.

A long-fin alternative is to use a soft weight belt with from 2 to 4 pounds (more if you wear a wetsuit)—just enough to help you get under the surface without using up all your energy. As you descend, you become neutrally buoyant at about 15-20 feet so you don't have to fight popping up. Of course, the sword cuts two ways, since you must swim up under your own power in time to breathe.

Into the Water

Getting Started

Now that you've assembled a nice collection of snorkel gear, you're ready to go! On a sunny tropical morning you're down at the water's edge. Little one-foot waves slap the sand lightly, while a soft warm breeze takes the edge off the intensity of the climbing sun. It's a great day to be alive and out in the water.

Going snorkeling, it's better to have no suntan lotion on your face or hands. You sure don't want it washing into your eyes to make them burn and water. Wear a nice big hat instead on your way to the water. You applied lotion to your back before you left, so it had time to become effective. Then you washed off your hands and rinsed them well so the lotion couldn't contaminate your mask later.

Or you could do like we do, and skip all the lotion. Being outside as much as we are, and in and out of the water, we prefer to carefully cover up instead—we find too much lotion hard on our skin. Big broad hats like your boat captain wears help. Comfortable cotton cover-ups look good and are cool. Lycra body suits or wetsuits in the water let you stay in for as long as you wish. Do watch out for reflected light on long boat trips, which can bounce off the water and sizzle your tender face.

convict tang

Checking Conditions

Take it nice and slow. Sit down and watch the waves for awhile. Check the slope of the beach. Consider whether there might be currents. Look for wave patterns, how big the biggest waves are and how far they wash up on the beach. When you see the pattern, you're ready to go. Set your gear down back well beyond the furthest watermarks on the sand. You don't want that seventh wave to sweep your gear away! Watch as long as it takes to be sure conditions aren't changing for the worse.

Gearing Up

Now defog the mask so that water vapor from your nose, or water leakage, won't bead up on your mask lens and spoil your view. There are several ways to defog that work well.

The classic solution is: SPIT. Spit on the inside of your dry mask lens, and rub it all around with your sunscreen-free finger. Step into the water, just out beyond the stirred up sand, and dip up a mask full of clear saltwater. Thoroughly rub and rinse off that spit, and dump the mask. Now you have prepared a mask that may be fog-resistant for the length of an average snorkel.

If you spit and polish, and still have fogging problems, there are several possible causes. Your mask may be gooped up with cosmetics, dried on saltwater residue or whatever other goo may be out there. A good cleaning with toothpaste may be in order (see Caring for Your Gear, page 24).

It's possible that you didn't actually wet all the surface with spit—perhaps because there were drops of water left on the lens. In that case, or if you just feel funny about spitting in your mask, you can use no-fog solution. It actually does work even better than spit. No-fog comes in small, handy, inexpensive bottles that seem to last forever because you use only a few drops at a time.

If you prefer to make your own, a mixture of half baby shampoo (so you don't irritate your eyes) and half water works fine. Some recipes add alcohol to the mix. Unless you are an excursion boat operator and use defog by the gallon, it's easier to just buy some!

Our favorite trick is to pre-apply no-fog solution to the dry masks as we load up our gear, and then let it dry. When you get to the water, just rinse out the mask thoroughly. This seems to last a long time.

Getting Comfortable

After you rinse your mask, try its fit. Adjust the mask strap and snorkel until they're comfortable. Hold the snorkel in your mouth without tightening your jaws. It can be quite loose without falling out. Putting your mask on long before you enter the water can cause it to fog from your exertions.

Getting Wet

Now retrieve your fins and walk back in the water, watching the waves carefully. NEVER turn your back on the ocean for long, lest a rogue wave sneak up on you and whack you good. The key is to stay alert and awake—especially on entry and exit.

If the bottom is sandy smooth, wade on out until you're about waist deep. Pull your mask on, making sure you remove any stray hair from under the edge. Position the snorkel in your mouth and start breathing. You can practice this in a pool or hot tub.

Duck down in the water so you're floating and pull on your fins just like sneakers. Be sure no sand is trapped in the fins. Make a smooth roll to your stomach, pause to float and relax until you're comfortable, and you're off! Flip those fins and you have begun your re-entry into the sea.

As you float, practice steady breathing through the snorkel. Breathe slowly and deeply. People sometimes tense up at first and take short breaths. When this happens, you're only getting stale air from the snorkel rather than lots of fresh air from outside. If you ever feel tired or out of breath, don't remove your mask. Just stop as long as necessary, float, breathe easy and relax.

After you've become quite comfortable breathing this way, check how your mask is doing. Make sure it isn't leaking. Adjust the strap if needed. And keep adjusting until it's just right. Slide your snorkel strap to a comfortable position, with the tube pointing about straight up as you float looking down at about a 30° angle.

Swimming while snorkeling is easy once you've relaxed. No arms are required. What works best is to hold your arms straight back along your sides, keep your legs fairly straight and kick those fins slowly without bending your knees much. Any swimming technique will work, of course, but some are more tiring. Practice using the least amount of energy. Once you learn how to snorkel the easy way,

Motion Sickness

Motion sickness (such as seasickness, carsickness or airsickness) is a minor inner ear disorder which can really cut into your pleasure on the water, on long, curvy road trips or in choppy air. Fortunately, motion sickness is quite controllable these days. All it takes is a little advance planning to turn a potentially miserable experience into a normal, fun one. Don't let old fears keep you from great water adventures anymore.

Mel can get seasick just by vividly imagining a rocking boat, so he has personally tried just about every remedy. These field trials are a messy business, so we'll spare you the details, and just pass on what really works in our experience.

Forget the wrist pressure-point bands—they don't do the job for anyone we've ever met. You might as well put them in the closet along with your ultrasonic pest repeller, in our opinion.

The most effective remedy we've found so far is Meclizine, a pill formerly available by prescription, but now over the counter. It works perfectly for Mel with no noticeable side effects. Alcohol can apparently interact with it to make you drowsy, though Mel has had a beer on excursions without falling asleep.

We learned about Meclizine when Jon Carroll, a columnist in the San Francisco Chronicle, reported that it had sufficed for him in 15-25 foot swell on the way to Antarctica. If it does the job there, it should handle all but the most radical of snorkeling excursions. It's always worked for us.

An over-the-counter alternative is Benadryl usually used as a decongestant. It can also be effective against motion sickness. Ginger is also claimed to be effective. As much as we enjoy ginger as a spice, we cannot substantiate that it helps at all.

Use these medicines carefully and only after consulting your doctor. In some cases, you must avoid alcohol, other drugs or diving, since these medications can produce drowsiness.

you can use all the power you like touring large areas as if you were a migrating whale. But if you're breaking the surface with your fins, going "splash, plunk, splash", you're wasting energy. Be cool and smooth and quiet as a fish, and you'll swim like a dolphin.

eyestripe surgeonfish

Clearing Your Mask

Eventually you will need to practice clearing your mask. If you have a purge valve, just blow out gently. The scuba method: take a deep breath, then tip your head up, but with the mask still under the surface. Press your palm to the top of the mask against your forehead, or hold your fingers on the top of the mask and exhale through your nose. This forces water out the bottom of the mask.

Taking It Easy

Relax and try not to push yourself too hard. Experienced snorkelers may urge you on faster than you're comfortable because they've forgotten how it feels to get started. As your experience builds, you'll find it easy too. It's like learning to drive a car. Remember how even a parking lot seemed like a challenge? It helps to practice your beginning snorkeling in a calm easy place—with a patient teacher. With a little persistence, you'll soon overcome your fears and be ready. Don't feel like you should rush. Play around and have fun!

Pacing

When you're having a good time, it's easy to forget and over-extend yourself. That next rocky point beckons, and then a pretty spot beyond that. Pretty soon, you're many miles from home and getting tired. Getting cold and overly tired can contribute to poor judgement in critical situations, making you more vulnerable to injury. Why risk turning your great snorkeling experience into a disaster? Learn your limits, and how to pace yourself.

Our favorite technique: If we plan on a one-hour snorkel, we watch the time and start heading back when we've been in the water 30 minutes. If the currents could run against us on the way back, we allow extra time and energy. We like to start our snorkel by swimming against the current, making the trip home surprisingly easy and quick.

If you're cruising along, making great time, pay extra attention. Rather than being a snorkeling superman all of a sudden, you may be drifting along with a fast current. Stop and check the drift by watching the coral below you, and plankton in the water. If there is a current, allow extra time/energy for swimming back against it. Or if you're towing your reef shoes along, sometimes you can enjoy the ride and walk back (assuming you're sure there's a good exit ahead). You can use your fins for shade.

Knowing Your Limits

Have you heard the old saloon saying: "Don't let your mouth write checks that your body can't cover"?

Let's paraphrase this as "Don't let your ego take you places your body can't get you back from." Consider carefully how well-conditioned your legs are, so you'll have enough reserve to be able to make it back home, and then some in case of an emergency.

Snorkeling Alone

In your enthusiasm for the reef, you may wind up in this situation: your significant other prefers watching sports on ESPN to snorkeling one afternoon, and you're sorely tempted to just head out there alone. Think twice. Snorkeling, done in buddy teams, is a pretty safe recreation, especially if conditions are favorable. Just as in scuba diving, having a buddy along reduces the risk of a small problem becoming a big problem or even a fatal problem. We won't spell out all the bad things that could happen; we trust your imagination.

Caring for Your Gear

You just had a great snorkeling experience—now you can thank the gear that helped make it possible, by taking good care of it.

Rinse and Dry

If there are beach showers, head right up and rinse off. Salt residue is sticky and corrosive. Rinse salt and sand off your wetsuit, fins, mask and snorkel before the saltwater dries. If you can, dry your gear in the shade. It's amazing how much damage sun can do to the more delicate equipment—especially the mask. When the sun odometer hits 100,000 miles, you can kiss those soft parts good-bye.

Safety Inspections

Keep an eye on vulnerable parts after a few years (strap, snorkel-holder, buckles). Parts are usually available in Hawai'i, but not in the middle of a snorkeling adventure unless you're on a very well-equipped excursion.

If you use any equipment with purge valves, watch for sand on the delicate little flap valves. Also replace them when they deteriorate. Masks and snorkels are useless when the valves give way. Most snorkels now have a purge valve at the bottom, and some masks.

Clean Your Mask

A mask needs a thorough cleaning between trips. Unless your mask instructions advise otherwise, use a regular, non-gel toothpaste to clean the lens inside and out, polishing off accumulated goo. Wash the toothpaste off with warm water, using your finger to clean it well.

peacock grouper

Sign Language

Any serious snorkeler should bother to learn some basic signs starting with some of the standard scuba ones such as OK —meaning "Are you OK?", which should be answered with another OK; *palm up* for "stop", *wobbling hand* for "problem", and *thumb down*, meaning "heading down" (in this case referring to surface diving). This is an essential safety issue making it possible to communicate even if slightly separated or underwater. See a few of the signs below.

It's also a nuisance to take the snorkel out of your mouth every time you want to say "Did you see that moray!?!" Worse yet is trying to understand your buddy who frantically gestures and mumbles through the snorkel while you play charades. With a frequent snorkeling companion it's fun to develop signs for the creatures you might see. Eel can be indicated by three fingers looking like an E or by a wavy line drawn in the water. Then all you have to do is point and there it is!

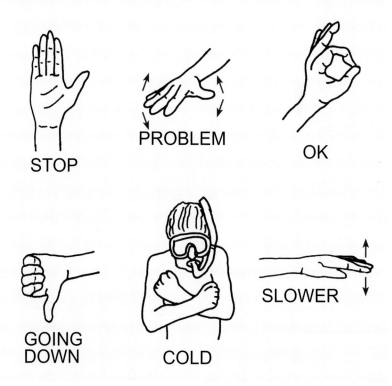

STOP

PROBLEM

OK

GOING
DOWN

COLD

SLOWER

Hazards

Life just isn't safe. Snorkeling has a few hazards that you should know and avoid if possible. You already know the dangers of car and air travel, yet you mustered your courage and decided that a trip to Hawai'i was worth the risks. You took reasonable precautions like buckling your seat belt. Well, if you're sensible about it, you're safer in the water than while driving to get to the water.

Some people are hesitant to snorkel because they imagine meeting a scary creature in the water. But wouldn't you rather be able to see what's down there when you're swimming? We much prefer to see whatever we might step on or run into. The realities are seldom scary, and often beautiful instead. Don't let exaggerated risks keep you from enjoying life to the fullest.

We don't think it makes sense to overemphasize certain lurid but unlikely dangers (such as sharks) and pay no attention to the more likely hazard of sunburn which causes more aggravation to tourists.

Sunburn

This is the worst medical problem you're likely to face—especially if you weren't blessed with genetically sun-resistant skin. Lycra suits are better for you and the environment than sunscreen. The top (or open) deck of a boat is a serious hazard to the easily-burned because bounced rays from the water will double your exposure. The best protection is covering up. Evidence mounts that sunscreen still allows skin damage even though it stops the burning. Thanks to ozone depletion, we can now get more sun in a given hour.

When snorkeling, omit sunscreen on your face or hands, because you'll be sorry later if you get the stuff in your eyes. It can really sting and make it difficult to see well enough to navigate back to shore. To avoid using sunscreen, we strongly recommend lycra body suits. Or simply wear some old clothing.

Take an old sun hat to leave on the beach with your gear bag, especially if you have to hike midday across a reflective white beach. Take old sunglasses that are not theft-worthy. If you must leave prescription glasses on the beach, use your old ones. Kailua is a great place to find amazingly cheap sunglasses and flip-flops, such as at Costco or Walmart. For long hours in the sun, look into the better sunglasses that filter more of the damaging rays.

Understanding Waves

Waves are travelling ripples in the water, mostly generated by wind blowing over large expanses of water. Having considerable energy, the waves keep going until something stops them. They may travel many thousands of miles before dissipating that energy. Here is the wellspring of the breaking surf. That beautiful surf can also be the biggest danger facing snorkelers.

Take time to sit on a high point and watch the waves approaching the coast, and you will see patterns emerge. Usually there is an underlying groundswell from one direction, waves that may have originated in distant storms. This is the main source of the rhythmical breaking waves, rising and falling in size in noticeable patterns. Sometimes there will be a smaller secondary groundswell from another direction. Often, there will be a series of small waves, followed by one or more larger waves, and the cycle repeats. Pay attention to the patterns and it will be less likely that you'll get caught by surprise.

Local winds add extra energy in their own directions. In Hawai'i, snorkeling is usually easiest in the mornings, before the daily winds create chop and larger waves. Most excursions head out early to make sure they have smooth sailing and calm snorkeling. Sometimes afternoon excursions are offered at reduced prices to compensate for expected rougher conditions.

Occasionally a set of larger waves or a single large rogue wave comes in with little or no warning. A spot that was protected by an offshore reef suddenly has breaking waves. This change can happen while you're out, and make coming back difficult.

Our single worst moment in many years of snorkeling and diving was at Po'ipū Beach Park in Kaua'i after Hurricane 'Iniki had scattered boulders under the water. We had no problem snorkeling around the boulders in a light swell, protected by the reef further out. Suddenly much larger waves crossed the reef and began breaking over us, sweeping everyone back and forth among and against the boulders. Ouch!

Since then we have been extra careful to avoid potentially hazardous situations. We always take time to study the waves before entering and ponder what would happen if they suddenly grew much larger, and what our strategy would be. Sometimes we just head for a calmer beach.

Rip Currents

Hawai'i does not have large barrier reefs to intercept incoming waves. Many of Hawai'i's beaches are exposed to the occasional powerful ocean swell—which is especially common in the winter or during storms.

Waves breaking against a shore push volumes of water up close to the shore. As this piles up, it has to flow back to the ocean, and often flows sideways along the shore until it reaches a convenient, often deeper-bottomed exit point. There, a fast, narrow river of water flows out at high speed. Rip currents, which can carry swimmers out quickly, are of limited duration by their very nature and usually stop no more than 100 yards out.

Sometimes it's possible to swim sideways, but often it's better to simply ride it out. Don't panic. Although the current might be very strong, it won't take you far or drown you, unless you exhaust

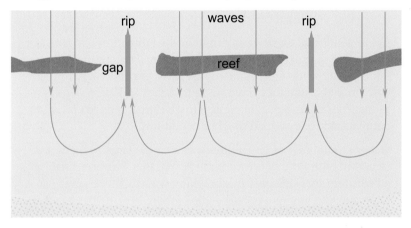

yourself by swimming against it. It's very easy to float in salt water until help arrives—assuming you're at a beach where someone can see you. Don't try to swim in through waves where there's any chance of being mashed on lava rocks or coral. Don't swim against the current to the point of exhaustion. When in doubt, float and conserve your energy, while you plan the safest way out.

Even at the most protected beaches all the water coming in must get out, so when swell is up, there's a current somewhere. Big waves beyond the breakwater may seem harmless, but the more water comes in, the more must get out. This is a good reason to ALWAYS wear fins even when the inner reef is calm.

Rip currents should not be confused with offshore currents, such as the infamous Tahiti Express. There are some major flows of water offshore that can be faster than you can swim even with fins. Do be alert and careful if you swim out beyond rocky points. Slowly test the direction you are moving when not swimming. Start your snorkel by swimming the more difficult direction, then you can coast back. Or travel swiftly with the current and send us a postcard from Tahiti.

Hypothermia

Open ocean water is always cooler than your body, and it cools you off more rapidly than the air. With normal exertion, your body still cools bit by bit. After awhile (perhaps 30-45 minutes) most of us start feeling chilly. Later, shivering begins. When your temperature drops even further, hypothermia sets in. When your body temperature has dropped enough, your abilities to move and even think become surprisingly impaired. It can sneak up on you.

We used to think hypothermia was just an interesting concept, until it happened to us after a long snorkel in some unusually cold water. We were shivering, but having a great time, and snorkeled on and on. Fortunately, we noticed the decrease in our co-ordination and headed in while we still could. You'd have laughed to see us stumbling clumsily out of the waves. We headed straight for the nearest jacuzzi (not recommended for full-blown hypothermia!). As we warmed up, our limbs tingled like fizzy water was going through our veins.

One of the first symptoms of hypothermia is poor judgement. Buddies can watch out for each other better than you can watch out for yourself alone—one example of the benefits of having a partner. Check up on each other often in cold water.

As soon as you are aware that you're cold, it's time to plan your way back. When shivering starts, you should head for shore immediately. Be particularly careful in situations requiring good judgement and skill to be safe, especially when diving, snorkeling at a remote beach, night snorkeling, dealing with waves, or when anticipating a difficult exit from the water.

In Hawai'i, it's usually easy to warm up rapidly since the air temperature is fairly warm at sea level. Even without hypothermia, it's good to warm up between snorkels. If you came by car, it will probably be nicely solar-heated by the time you return. We take gallon milk jugs of warm water to rinse off with at no-shower spots.

Sea Urchins

Probably the most common critter injury is stepping on a spiny sea urchin and walking away with lots of spines under your skin. The purple-black spiny sea urchins with long spines tend to appear in groups and favor shallow water, so watch carefully if you see even one—it probably has friends. Full-foot flippers or booties help a lot, but don't guarantee protection. Watch where you put your hands—especially in shallow water.

Many folks recommend seeing a doctor for urchin spine slivers. Others prefer to just let the spines fester and pop out weeks later. Remove as much spine as you can. Vinegar (or other acidic liquid) will make it feel better. Soaking in Epsom salts helps and the small spines will dissolve in a few weeks, but definitely see a doctor at any sign of infection. Don't wait for blood poisoning to set in!

banded sea urchin

Barracuda

The great barracuda can grow to two meters, has sharp teeth and strong jaws, and swims like a torpedo. For years Judy had removed earrings before swimming after hearing rumors that they attract barracuda, but we've uncovered absolutely no confirming reports of severed earlobes attributable to jewelry. But they can bite!

Barracudas are capable of seriously injuring a swimmer so should be taken seriously. Those teeth are just as sharp as they look. Barracudas appear to have attitude, and apparently sometimes do. Our own preference is to respect their territory and allow them some space. Other varieties of barracuda such as the smaller Heller's barracuda appear more innocuous. Appearances can deceive, however.

Once a four-foot great barracuda swam directly beneath us in the Caribbean and appeared annoyed that we were invading his home territory (or so we thought from the fierce look on

great barracuda

his face). A usually calm and steady German surgeon headed up the nearest rocks as if she could fly. The rest of us snorkeled by him repeatedly with no problem, but didn't appreciate the look he gave us. We later came to realize that they always look grumpy, but seldom literally bite, like some folks you may know. Perhaps the bigger danger comes from eating the delicious barracuda meat, sometimes containing ciguatera, which is a potent neurotoxin.

Sea Jellies

The Portuguese man-of-war floats on top, looking like a sail fin one to four inches in size, with long stinging filaments that are quite painful. Stay out of the water if you see one. Even avoid dead ones on the sand! They're very pretty in lovely shades of purple, but can cause severe pain.

sea jelly

Vinegar or unseasoned meat tenderizer helps ease the sting and helps stop the release of venom from the stinging cells if tentacles are clinging to you. Use wet sand as a last resort. If you feel ill, see a doctor right away. If sea jellies are present, locals will know which ones are harmful. Sea jellies have not been a problem for us in Hawai'i. In all our years in the water, we've only been stung by a Portuguese man-of-war once, not in Hawai'i, and it wasn't serious.

A reader recently reported getting little nips that were annoying. These could have been bits of hydroids floating around, or possibly small stinging sea jellies. Wearing a wetsuit or lycra would have taken care of that. Generally, these little nips have no long lasting effects, so it's best to not panic. Do avoid rubbing bare skin against mooring ropes, which often are covered with hydroids.

Rays

Sting rays prefer to avoid you, but hang out on the bottom where they're easy to step on. They prefer resting in calm water that is slightly warmer than the surrounding area—just the areas favored by people for swimming. Step on them and they may sting you, so the injury is usually to the foot or ankle. They can inflict a serious or painful sting to people—especially children. It's best to get immediate first aid and follow up with medical assistance.

In this case snorkelers have an advantage over swimmers because snorkelers can see sting rays and easily avoid them. In Maui we once saw them swim between children's legs in shallow water at Kapalua

cleaner wrasse on spotted eagle ray

Bay and were amazed to see how adept the rays were at avoiding people. They really try to steer clear.

Manta rays don't sting, but they're much larger. They are often six to eight feet across, weighing several hundred pounds. They maneuver beautifully, so they don't pose any danger. With a little luck and some planning, you may see one of these beautiful creatures.

Poisonous Fish

Lionfish (also called turkeyfish) and scorpionfish have spines which are very poisonous. Don't step on or touch them! Their poison can cause serious pain and infection or allergic reaction, so definitely see a doctor if you have a close, personal encounter with one. Fins or booties can help protect your tender feet.

Mel Malinowski

lionfish

Scorpionfish can blend in so well along the bottom in shallow water that they're easy to miss. Lionfish, however, are colorful and easy to spot. Since these fish are not abundant in Hawai'i, they are treasured sightings for snorkelers. You are not likely to see one while shallow-water snorkeling.

Eels

Eels are rarely aggressive and often tamed by divers. Most do possess a formidable array of teeth, which should be avoided. An eel bite can definitely cause serious bleeding requiring prompt medical attention. Another reason not to snorkel alone!

whitemouth moray eel

33

Eels are fascinating and easy to find in Hawai'i. Count on eels to make every effort to avoid you, so there's no need to panic at the sight of one—even if it's swimming freely. Eels aren't interested in humans as food, but they do want to protect themselves and can usually do so with ease by slipping away into the nearest hole. Do we need to warn you to keep your hands out of crevices in the coral?

Cone Shells

The snails inside these pretty black and brown-decorated shells can fire a poisonous dart. The venom can cause a serious reaction or even death—especially to allergic persons. If in doubt, head for a doctor. If you never pick up underwater shells, you should be OK.

Drowning

Not likely to happen to you, but we want to help you become so alert and prepared that you have a safe vacation. Accidental drowning is a very preventable tragedy.

We looked up the statistics for the past 30 years, and they are both comforting and cautionary. An average of 60 folks drown each year in all of Hawai'i. A much lower number than fatalities from auto wrecks, industrial accidents, or probably even accidents around the home, but not a group you want to join.

A couple things stand out about who are the victims. Half of the victims are visitors. Not too surprising, since you assume locals are more aware of the hazards. But 80% are males, mostly 20 to 50 years old! You'd think this would be a low-risk group with adequate swimming skills.

What leads these fellows to get into a dangerous situation? Well, some guys just can't help overrating their athletic prowess, and perhaps underestimating the power of the ocean.

Some locations seem distinctly more hazardous. Beautiful Waipio Valley in the north can be calm as glass one day and great surfing the next. South swell can pick up in the summer making most of the beaches along the west fairly unpredictable.

It's easy to swim and snorkel in the island of Hawai'i safely. Improve your odds by checking which way the swell is rolling and picking protected beaches when the surf is pounding. Don't overestimate your stamina, or swim alone. Perhaps you might also follow our personal rule: always wear fins when swimming in the open ocean in Hawai'i—no matter how calm the water seems!

Sharks

Sharks are seldom a problem for snorkelers—people are not on their menu unless mistaken for legitimate prey or really obnoxious tourists. In Hawai'i deaths average less than one in two years with surfers the most common target because they look like seals. Sharks hunt in murky river runoff, but most snorkelers avoid these conditions anyway (our recommendation, too).

Statisticians tell us that you're more likely to be killed by a pig, dog or bee than a shark. We take great comfort in that, as I'm sure you do, too; though we've quit eating bacon just in case.

Mel Malinowski

blacktip reef shark

Some people will suggest you can pet, feed or even tease certain types of shark. We personally give sharks a bit of respect and leave them entirely in peace. Most sharks are well-fed on fish and not all that interested in ordinary tourists, but it's hard to tell by looking at a shark whether it has had a bad day.

Sharks mostly feed late in the late afternoon or at night, causing some people to prefer to enjoy the water more in the morning or midday. If you're in an area frequented by sharks, this might be good to keep in mind. We must admit that we snorkel at any hour, and occasionally night snorkel, and have had no problems.

In Hawai'i, with luck, you might possibly see sandbar, black-tip reef, white-tip reef or even hammerhead sharks—more often in deep water sites like Kealakekua Bay or near harbors. Of these, only hammerhead sharks should be avoided. Unless you're a surfer or swim FAR out from shore, your chances of ever seeing a tiger shark are very slim.

Snorkeling Sites

Where are those big beautiful fish?

In the site section ahead, you'll find snorkeling site reviews organized from the far north of the island of Hawai'i, proceeding in counter-clockwise direction, with more details about our favorites as well as those with special appeal, such as good beginner beaches.

Some sites are surprisingly difficult to find and many require poorly marked hikes, so bring these maps with you. People often drive up and down the highways with no idea which spots to try for snorkeling. Some look plausible, but have little coral or fish, while other great sites are well-concealed underwater, and you'd never guess that they are there. Some visitors even think this island lacks good beaches—not knowing that there are beaches in South Kohala that have been rated as among the best in the world! Signs are sometimes scarce and small, so we've included maps and directions to help you find every spot.

Whatever your level of swimming or snorkeling ability, you can find a great spot to enjoy yourself along the west coast of Hawai'i. When staying in the east, there are a few other sites farther afield (such as Richardson) that are worth a try. It's not possible to snorkel all the excellent sites in a week, so we hope that Snorkel Hawai'i, the Big Island, will help you select a satisfying sample of the diverse snorkeling opportunities available here.

When selecting a site, always consider direction of the swell. If the local paper says eight foot north swell, stay away from bays that face north. The west side of the island of Hawai'i is pretty well shielded from north to northwest swell by O'ahu and Maui. When the swell comes from the south, you might find those northern bays calm as bath water.

Conditions can change suddenly out here in the Pacific, so come to Hawai'i prepared to be flexible. When distant storms or local winds bring iffy conditions to some Hawai'ian sites, check this book for sites that offer relatively calm conditions year round. There are definitely beaches here that are calm all but a few days each year.

We begin this site section in the far north of the island beyond the town of Hāwī, where the highway ends at Pololu Valley. Then we continue counter-clockwise around the island, ending at Waipi'o

Valley, where the highway ends again. You'll quickly notice that we describe far more sites on the west side of the island. That's because the west offers more protected beaches with better access and is where the large majority of tourists choose to stay.

The largest concentration of good sites stretches from South Kohala, through North Kona, Kailua/Keauhou, and South Kona. The South Kohala Area offers large sand beaches (Hāpuna and 'Anaeo'omalu, often called A-Bay), great snorkeling after a long hike (Makaīwa), a short hike (Kauna'oa), shallow enough for kids (Pāhoa) and a two-mile long reef to explore (Puakō). And more!

The North Kona Area offers much of the same with remote beauty (Makalawena), tiny cove (Honokōhau Harbor), long reef (Old Airport), and Baby Beach.

The Kailua/Keauhou Area has many small coves tucked into the coral shoreline with Kahalu'u being the most famous and now quite crowded, but still worth a snorkel.

The South Kona Area offers a couple of the best snorkeling sites on the island (Kealakekua and Two Step at Hōnaunau), although the first is difficult to access except by boat or kayak.

The South Area (south end of the island rather than South Kona, which is further north) has some more good sites that are worth checking out, but are more affected by south swell—particularly in the summer. Mahana Bay (Green Sand) and Punalu'u (Black Sand) are both beautiful and sometimes offer safe snorkeling. Whittington is a bit more protected.

The East Area is mostly exposed to the prevailing northeast trades, so is often too rough, however we've listed several sites that are more protected. Richardson near Hilo offers good snorkeling while surfing is popular beyond the protected area. Wai'ōpae Tidepools are almost completely protected from the open ocean—more like salt water swimming pools. Isaac Hale can also be quite calm on a good day.

The Big Island of Hawai'i has the largest number of good snorkeling sites, as well as the greatest diversity of any Hawai'ian island, and more reliable quality snorkeling. We highly recommend it to snorkeling enthusiasts—both beginners and hard-core. That's a big part of why this island became our home and we hope you enjoy it as much as we do. While in Hawai'i, help us take care of this precious resource. Malama Hawai'i (translation: take care of Hawai'i).

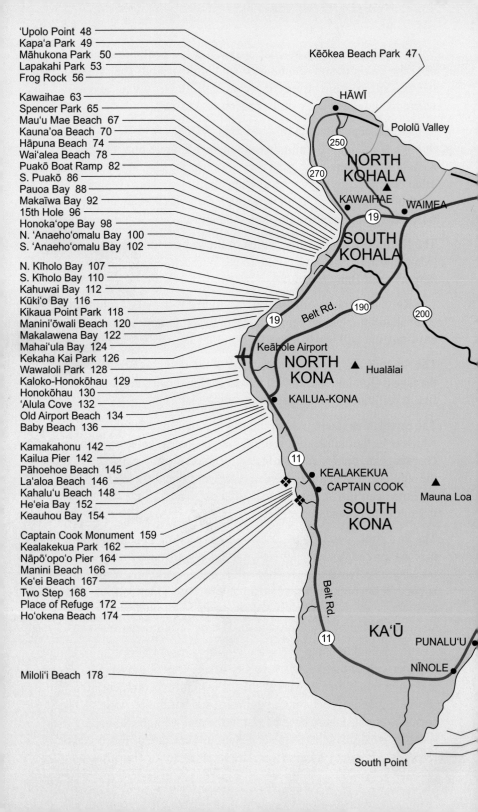

HĀWĪ

Pololū Valley

250

270

NORTH
KOHALA

KAWAIHAE

WAIMEA

19

SOUTH
KOHALA

Belt Rd.

19

190

200

Keāhole Airport

NORTH
KONA

▲ Hualālai

KAILUA-KONA

11

KEALAKEKUA

CAPTAIN COOK

▲
Mauna Loa

SOUTH
KONA

Belt Rd.

KA'Ū

PUNALU'U

NĪNOLE

11

South Point

Snorkel Site Index Map

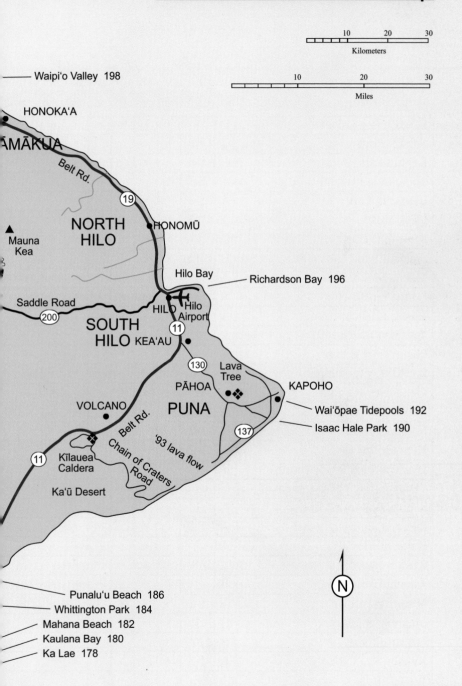

10 20 30
Kilometers

10 20 30
Miles

Waipi'o Valley 198

HONOKA'A

ĀMĀKUA

Belt Rd.

19

NORTH
HILO

HONOMŪ

Mauna
Kea

Hilo Bay

Richardson Bay 196

Saddle Road
200

HILO Hilo
Airport

SOUTH
HILO KEA'AU

11

130

Lava
Tree

PĀHOA

KAPOHO

VOLCANO

PUNA

Wai'ōpae Tidepools 192
Isaac Hale Park 190

Belt Rd.

137

'93 lava flow

Chain of Craters Road

Kīlauea
Caldera

Ka'ū Desert

11

N

Punalu'u Beach 186
Whittington Park 184
Mahana Beach 182
Kaulana Bay 180
Ka Lae 178

Sites at a Glance

	Snorkeling	Entry	Sandy beach	Restroom	Showers	Picnic area	Scenic	Shade
Keōkea Beach Park	C	1	•	•	•	•	•	•
'Upolu Point	C	1-3					•	•
Kapa'a Park	C	1-3	•	•		•	•	
Māhukona Park	A	1-3		•		•	•	
Lapakahi Park	A	2-3		•			•	
Frog Rock	A	1-3					•	
Kawaihae Harbor	B	1	•	•	•	•	•	•
Spencer Park	B	1	•	•	•	•	•	•
Mau'u Mae Beach	A	1	•				•	•
Kauna'oa Beach (Mauna Kea)	A	1	•	•	•	•	•	
Hāpuna Beach	A	1-3	•	•	•	•	•	•
Wai'alea Beach (69)	A	1	•	•	•	•	•	•
Puakō Boat Ramp	A	1	•				•	
Puakō Bay (south end)	A	1-2			•	•	•	
Pauoa Bay (Orchid)	B	1	•	•	•	•	•	•
Makaīwa Bay (Mauna Lani)	A	1	•	•	•		•	•
Fifteenth Hole	A	1-2					•	
Honoka'ope Bay	B	1-2	•	•			•	•
'Anaeho'omalu Bay (north)	B	1	•	•	•		•	•
'Anaeho'omalu Bay (south)	C	1	•	•	•	•	•	•
Kīholo Bay (north)	A	1	•			•	•	•
Kīholo (south)	A	1-2	•	•		•	•	•
Kahuwai Bay	A	1	•	•	•		•	•
Kūki'o Bay	C	1	•	•	•	•	•	•
Kikaua Point Park	B	1	•	•	•	•	•	•
Manini'ōwali Beach	A	1-2	•	•	•	•	•	
Makalawena Bay	B	1	•			•	•	•
Mahai'ula Bay	B	1	•	•		•	•	•
Kekaha Kai Park	A	1-3	•	•			•	•
Wawaloli Park		3		•	•	•	•	•

A	Excellent	1	Easy
B	Good	2	Moderate
C	Fair	3	Difficult

Page	Map page	
47	46	tiny calm area for quick dip, few fish or coral
48	46	enter from rocks only when calm, very secluded
49	45	high tide best for clearance, rocky beach, no crowds
50	51	ladder entry near parking lot, easy when calm
53	55	interesting park, good reef, dangerous when rough
56	57	extensive & interesting reef, very secluded, short hike
63	64	extensive protected area, but not many fish
65	64	big family park, reef extends far, scattered coral heads
67	69	secluded, gorgeous beach, need pass, short hike
70	71	gorgeous beach, come early for pass, short hike
74	75	popular big park, often rough in winter & afternoons
78	79	delightful & easy when calm, pretty bay with shade
82	83	swim out long boat channel to best snorkeling
86	83	broad shallow reef, swim along edge (not over)
88	89	facilities at park, hike to Orchid for snorkeling
92	93	3/4 mile hike from parking, extensive & varied reef
96	93	long hike from parking, poke around fingers of reef
98	93	"black" sand, close to public parking, uncrowded
100	101	long hike from parking, long swim to clear water
102	101	popular long beach, all water sports, murky water
107	108	shallow, lovely bay, turtles, half hour sunny hike
110	108	high tide best, reef near shore, usually uncrowded
112	113	best early mornings, must hike from public parking
116	115	snorkeling channel at far south end of shallow bay
118	115	very shallow, protected cove & access to south Kūki'o
120	105	beautiful broad soft sandy beach, snorkel either end
122	127	beautiful, secluded, rough lava hike from Kekaha Kai
124	127	beautiful, fairly secluded, short hike from Kekaha Kai
126	127	often rougher than nearby beaches, but lots of coral
128	105	very deep water, usually too rough, best for picnic

Sites at a Glance

	Snorkeling	Entry	Sandy beach	Restroom	Showers	Picnic area	Scenic	Shade
Honokōhau Harbor	C	1-2	•	•	•	•	•	•
'Alula Cove	B	1	•	•	•	•	•	•
Pāwai Bay (Old Airport)	B	1-2	•			•	•	•
Baby Beach		1	•				•	•
Kamakahonu Beach	B	1	•				•	•
Kailua Pier	B	1-2	•				•	•
Pāhoehoe Park	B	1-3	•			•	•	•
La'aloa Beach (White Sands)	B	1-3	•	•	•	•	•	•
Kahalu'u Beach Park	A	1	•	•	•	•	•	•
He'eia Bay	B	1-2						•
Keauhou Bay	B	1		•	•	•	•	
Kealakekua (Cook Monument)	A	1					•	
Kealakekua Park	B	1-3		•	•	•	•	•
Nāpō'opo'o Pier	B	1				•	•	•
Manini Beach Park	B	1-2				•	•	•
Ke'ei Beach	B	2-3	•			•	•	•
Hōnaunau Bay (Two Step)	A	1-2		•		•	•	•
Place of Refuge (picnic area)	A	2-3		•		•	•	•
Ho'okena Beach	B	2	•	•	•	•	•	•
Miloli'i Beach Park	B	2	•			•	•	•
Ka Lae (South Point)	C	3					•	
Kaulana Bay	B	1	•				•	•
Mahana Beach (Green Sands)	B	1-3	•				•	
Whittington Beach Park	B	1-2	•	•	•	•	•	•
Punalu'u (Black Sand Beach)	C	2-3	•	•	•	•	•	•
Pohoiki (Isaac Hale Beach)	B	1	•	•	•	•	•	•
Wai'ōpae Tidepools	A	1					•	
Richardson Beach Park	A	1-2		•	•	•	•	•
Waipi'o Valley	C	3	•				•	•

A	Excellent	1	Easy
B	Good	2	Moderate
C	Fair	3	Difficult

Page	Map page	
130	131	secluded, tiny & shallow, high tide necessary
132	131	tiny, protected cove, snorkel beyond point when calm
134	135	when calm seas, snorkel wide area along coast
136	135	well-protected, but very shallow, good for small kids
142	143	central location, easy access to coast when calm
142	143	surprisingly good if you swim north, must avoid boats
145	139	lava shoreline, snorkel only when unusually calm
146	139	good when calm, but Kahalu'u usually calmer
148	149	VERY popular, large fish & turtles, damaged coral
152	153	small, protected, somewhat shallow, no crowds
154	153	good with few boats, best out toward either point
159	161	spectacular location, boat or kayak access, dolphins
162	163	rocky beach, but good snorkeling to left near lava
164	163	easy entry from pier when calm, extensive area
166	163	rocky beach, access Kelalakekua Bay when high tide
167	157	very rough road, exposed ocean with waves to cross
168	169	access from lava steps, 10-30' deep, diverse, the best!
172	169	entry from lava shelf when calm, experienced only
174	157	wide & shallow reef, poor facilities, need calm seas
178	5	semi-private Hawai'ian Lands area, best from boat
178	177	often VERY rough with currents, access by boat best
180	177	bare area, but good snorkel when low south swell
182	183	2-mile sunny hike, best with no south swell, beautiful
184	185	several beaches & tidepools, only if south swell low
186	185	black sand beach, rocky & often dangerous
190	193	enter near pier when seas calm, warm pools nearby
192	193	unique tidepools, no fins needed, treat with care
196	197	rocky, but protected, large area to explore, cooler
198	5	rarely calm enough, but spectacular, secluded location

North Kohala Area

Few tourists explore the farthest points in North Kohala, so it remains a charming, noncommercial corner of the island. Towns are small, the ocean is often rougher here, and the landscape ranges from bone dry to lush. 10,023-foot Haleakalā volcano on Maui looms just 29 miles across the channel. No big hotels or condos and little traffic here, just a varied drive to the end of Highway 270 at the beautiful Pololū Valley Lookout. Stop in the little town of Hāwī for lunch and visit quiet Keōkea Beach Park while you're up this way.

You can return by way of Highway 250 through the upcountry of the Kohala Mountains to the town of Waimea, lying at the foot of dramatic green hills, pasture land for Parker Ranch.

If you want to count on being able to enjoy the water, check surf conditions before heading to North Kohala on a long day trip. The north-facing sites are commonly too rough for safe water sports, especially in the winter. The west side of North Kohala is a better bet—especially protected Māhukona, arid, dramatic Lapakahi Park, and rather rocky Kapaʻa Beach.

We've listed snorkeling sites starting at the far north of the island, where swell is often high, good for surfing but not for swimming. Conditions become more favorable for snorkeling as we continue counter-clockwise around the Big Island of Hawaiʻi, with the most reliable snorkeling found in the areas of South Kohala, North Kona, Kailua to Keauhou and South Kona.

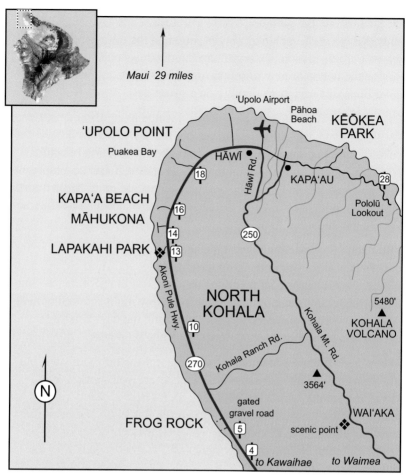

Maui 29 miles

'Upolo Airport
Pāhoa Beach
KĒŌKEA PARK

'UPOLO POINT
Puakea Bay
HĀWĪ
(18)
Hāwī Rd.
KAPA'AU
(28)

KAPA'A BEACH
MĀHUKONA
(16)
Pololū Lookout

(14)
(250)
LAPAKAHI PARK
(13)

NORTH KOHALA
5480'
KOHALA VOLCANO

Akoni Pule Hwy.
(10)
Kohala Mt. Rd.

(270)
Kohala Ranch Rd.
3564'

N

gated gravel road
WAI'AKA
FROG ROCK
(5)
scenic point

(4)
to Kawaihae   to Waimea

Map Symbols

Peak	▲
Place of interest	❖
Highway	——
Paved road	——
Minor paved road	——
Gravel road	–·–·–·
Foot path	- - - - -
Road number	(50)
Highway mileage marker	⛔11

Shower	⌐
Location of picture	≋⌐
Hotel or condominium	H
Parking area	P
Restroom	WC
Lava	🪨
Sand	▦
City	●

On a calm day, the west coast of North Kohala has several excellent sites. All are quite secluded, so you might be the only people in the water. For this reason, we urge extra caution, especially if you're new to the island or new to snorkeling. Each site is unique, so water conditions can vary considerably on a given day.

One of our favorite sites is Frog Rock, located along this coast. Large swell can make the entry dangerous, but flat water makes it easy enough for a beginner. The hike is short and the location beautiful, so check it out when you're up this way. Pending home development may eliminate access from the highway. Lapakahi Park, further north on the dry side, is also worth the drive—for the snorkel as well as a visit to the historical park.

Māhukona Bay, although near Lapakahi, offers a different snorkeling experience. Here you enter from a short ladder and snorkel within an old harbor area. Look for pieces of the wreck of the SS Kaua'i—big anchor chain links and boiler pieces. We enjoy night snorkeling here, spotting creatures that rarely come out during the day. You might even get to swim near mantas feeding on plankton here.

When conditions are favorable, try some of these northern sites, but always watch awhile to assess the swell before you snorkel. Early risers almost always get the calmest water. There is plenty of light for snorkeling by 7 a.m., and the water is often flat, calm and beautiful then. By 10-11 a.m., the wind-driven swell may come up, and it's a whole different snorkeling experience. We begin our tour with the park closest to the north end of the road.

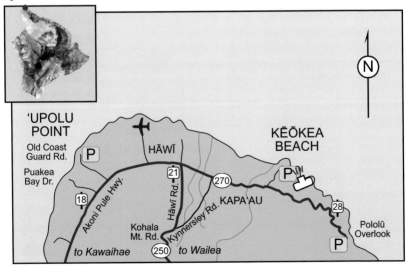

Kēōkea Beach Park

A quiet spot for a picnic in the far north, but you will rarely be able to snorkel outside of the narrow protected area that has no coral. This site catches the common wind-driven swell from the northeast, and even bigger swell in the winter. Good for a quick dip to cool off, but don't wander out into the open ocean waves and currents. A narrow channel at the east end of the bay is usually completely calm, but not large enough for much snorkeling. Portapotties, plenty of picnic tables, and a shower are available. There's a nice view of Maui and the choppy channel from the "upstairs" covered table. This park is open 7 a.m. to 11 p.m.

GETTING THERE   Heading north from Kailua-Kona on Highway 19, continue north on Highway 270 near Kawaihae Harbor. Continue past Hāwī and Kapaʻau unless you want to shop or eat in one of these beautiful towns. As you pass mile marker 27, watch on your left. You'll see a sign for the Kēōkea turnoff to your left. Follow the signs down toward the ocean for exactly a mile and you'll find the park at the end of the road. Park at the far right end of the lot (where it's unpaved) if you want to be near the calm channel.

'Upolu Point

Continuing counterclockwise, we begin to enter the area where seas are calmer more of the year. 'Upolu Point Coast Guard Station is located next to a public "beach" less than two miles from Highway 270. This site is somewhat protected from swell by two points and the fact that it faces west. While it has no beach, only large rocks, there's a fairly large area to explore when the sea is calm.

The access road is paved, but full of potholes. It's OK to drive with passenger cars as long as you don't mind a bit of bouncing. Parking is available at the end of the road to the left, while the gated coast guard station is found on the right. No facilities, sand, or shade and often better for fishing than swimming. Still, the reef can be seen from the parking lot and the water is often calm. Stay away from any waves breaking against the rocks.

GETTING THERE   Follow Highway 19 north to Kawaihae Harbor, then continue north on Highway 270 past Kapa'a Park. Watch for mile marker 18, then continue on .7 miles and turn onto Old Coast Guard Rd. Take this bumpy road two miles to the end, next to the gated coast guard buildings. Park in the lot to your left and either walk down the trail (on your far left) or climb over rocks in front. You'll be able to see both to decide. Snorkel between the parking lot and the point to the left. Do not snorkel beyond the far point because the current can be strong even on a seemingly calm day. This pretty bay can often be sheltered from wind and swell, but can also catch heavy surf at times, especially in the winter. At those times, it's better to head back to South Kohala for safe snorkeling.

Kapa'a Park

Located near the Big Island's far north, just a short hop from Highway 270, Kapa'a Park is the next site on our list as we proceed counter-clockwise. Most sites further north than Kapa'a Park are less likely to offer safe snorkeling in most weather. Kapa'a itself is often uncomfortably rough, and should be skipped if questionable. On a calm day, the snorkeling can be surprisingly easy.

Kapa'a Park includes a small, somewhat protected bay with a rocky black and white "beach" and hardly any sand. Facilities include a small parking lot, picnic tables and portapotties, but no drinking water. There's also a large covered picnic shelter on the right. A very basic, uncrowded park. Snorkeling is good—best if you snorkel to the left and beyond the point, water conditions permitting.

Summer is the best time to find easy swimming here because winter swell can make this part of the North Kohala coast hazardous. Mornings are nearly always calmer, with wind picking up by noon. When swell is low, you can snorkel south along the cliff as far as you like, exploring small coves along the way. You might see an octopus among the rocks if you look very closely and are lucky.

GETTING THERE

Head north on Highway 19, then stay left on Highway 270 near Kawaihae Harbor. Follow the signs to Māhukona. Kapa'a is located at mile marker 16 just north of Māhukona (see map, page 45). Turn makai (toward the ocean) on the narrow, winding one-lane road and drive .7 of a mile to the end. You can't miss the little park.

Māhukona Park

Less than a mile north of Lapakahi, you'll find this small park with a boat launch, ample parking, restrooms, picnic tables, but no beach, no shower and no drinking water. Snorkeling and swimming access are from a ladder down into about five feet of water, with the sand sloping out to about twenty feet deep.

The ladder is straight in front of parking. Don't attempt to swim or snorkel here when heavy swell arrives in the winter. We snorkeled in water calm enough for a 3-year-old, but the next day a young man died after being swept into the lava rocks by heavy swell. Even low swell can really sweep past the steps as they funnel into the shallow inner area. Nothing like trying to snag the ladder as you zip on by! At most times, you'll be OK if you don't go landward of the ladder.

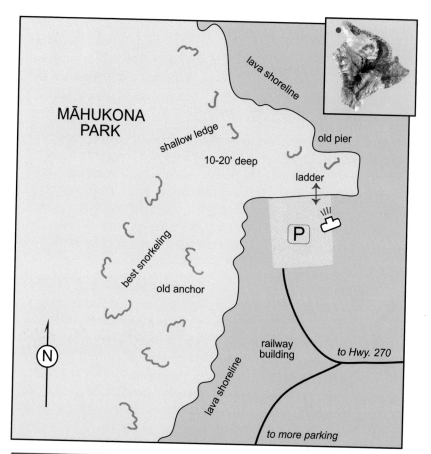

MĀHUKONA PARK

lava shoreline

shallow ledge

10-20' deep

old pier

ladder

best snorkeling

old anchor

P

railway building

lava shoreline

to Hwy. 270

to more parking

N

octopus

If you're planning to snorkel anywhere in North Kohala, check the wave reports before you drive this far. Māhukona is not as pristine as nearby Lapakahi, but access is much easier. The park is small and uncrowded, with easy entry just steps from your car. Māhukona is primarily a boulder habitat, but has a fair amount of coral patches, with plenty of big fish and good variety.

Snorkeling to either the north or south will take you over some relics from the steamship "Kaua'i" that sank here in 1913. Hefty anchor chains stretch across the bottom. We encountered an unusually bold octopus in the shallower area near the ladder. It displayed nearly every color and texture in its repertoire, and didn't attempt to hide. Larger fish frequent this site, so watch for bigeye emperor fish (moi) and bluefin trevally (ulua). On weekends this is a popular family fishing and swimming spot.

We like Māhukona for night snorkeling and have seen mantas here as well as unusual creatures that come out only at night. If you're lucky, the mantas will do somersaults in your light as they scoop up the plankton into their huge mouths. Bring friends and lots of dive lights because it's spooky with just one or two lights. When you first enter the water it looks entirely abandoned, but keep watching because you will eventually find some unusual creatures. Be alert for conger eels, 7-11 crabs, slipper lobsters, squid, and other reef dwellers that prefer to hide during the day. They don't seem to mind your light at night.

If you snorkel at Lapakahi, nearby Māhukona Park provides a convenient spot to picnic. Consider a day trip that takes you past Hāwī, to the end of Highway 270 to see the Pololū Valley, then back through upcountry Wailea. You may also enjoy a stop at scenic Keōkea Beach Park, but the north-facing coast is usually far too rough for snorkeling. Keōkea does have all facilities and a shallow, sheltered area to the right that provides a safe spot for a cooling dip.

GETTING THERE
Head north on Highway 19, then continue to the left on Highway 270 near Kawaihae Harbor (see area map, page 61). Watch for Lapakahi on your left, then go another .9 of a mile to the Māhukona sign between mile markers 14 and 16, at mile 14.9. Head toward the ocean for .4 of a mile, and you'll come to a T at the Hawai'i Railroad building (from an old sugarcane railway ending here). The parking lot and boat launch are to the right, while the rest of the park with no water access is to the left. The ladder is directly in front of the parking lot (see site map, page 51).

Lapakahi Park

Lapakahi Marine Life Conservation District and State Historical Park has a serene, somewhat austere beauty. Off the beaten track in North Kohala, it can seem abandoned in the winter. Lapakahi has no running water or showers and little shade on the trail, but there is usually a cooler of drinking water available.

When you park, stop by the office to check in with the park rangers. They strive to make sure everyone treats the park with respect. The rules include no towels or clothing left on the beach and no snorkeling to the left where there are important burial sites. It's OK to leave shoes, hats and glasses, since all are needed to hike down to the beach. And, please, no sunscreen in the water and no fish feeding. These are getting to be common requests in areas that wisely attempt to protect the natural diversity of reef life.

A 300-yard hike takes you directly down to the water—a worthwhile hike even if you don't swim. The trail is on the side of moderate hill with only a few small trees. While the trail isn't well marked, it's easy to see the beach. As you near the shore and intersect the main trail parallel to the shore, jog left and enter at the small pebble "beach." Snorkel to the right, but only if conditions are calm.

The water to your left is off-limits to the public out of respect for these ancient Hawai'ian grave sites.

Lapakahi has good fish populations, but not a lot of coral, with no showers and a fair access hike with no shade. Entry is across rocks, so don't enter if there's any problem with swell. It can be very tricky getting back out if big waves pick up. Early mornings are better here, since the wind usually picks up late morning.

Good swimming skills and fins are essential. Don't venture too far from shore since the currents can be strong. This is a place where you need to sit and watch for awhile. Also, ask park rangers for advice, but keep in mind they may be much better swimmers than you are. Wave size often varies in noticeable cycles, but may also change suddenly (see Understanding Waves, page 27). We snorkeled here one morning when the water was completely calm and thoroughly enjoyed the snorkeling as well as the atmosphere. For the entire hour we were the only visitors to the park.

Marine life is protected and the fish seem to understand, so they are unusually bold. We have seen huge schools of yellow tangs, an octopus, little juvenile yellowtail coris, and most of the usual reef fish. The coral is quite healthy, but does get a pounding in the winter.

Lapakahi is the site of a 13th century fishing village called Koai'a, abandoned in the 1800s when water was diverted for use at the sugar plantations. Stone foundations are all around you and it's now a hot, dry, but beautiful site. It's hard to compare lovely sites, but this is definitely a dramaticly austere one. Sit and imagine what it might have been like to live and work in this village when there was more rainfall, and before water was diverted for the sugar cane plantations. When swell is too high, consider trying Māhukona instead, but do visit Lapakahi Park at least once. The Lapakahi Park gate is open from 8 a.m. to 4 p.m.

GETTING THERE   Go north on Highway 19 (see map, page 61), past mile marker 68, and then turn left on Highway 270 near the harbor. You're at mile marker 2 on this road. Watch immediately for a Y (at a gas station) and continue on 270 (the right of the Y) heading north toward Mahukona. Follow 270 (Akuni Pule Highway) north to the Lapakahi sign on the left. It's between mile markers 13 and 14. Notice that they lock the gate at 4 p.m. and the sign suggests that if locked in, you may have to hike 7 and 1/2 miles north to the nearest phone! The total distance from the Kailua-Kona Junction to the Lapakahi turnoff is 46.6 miles.

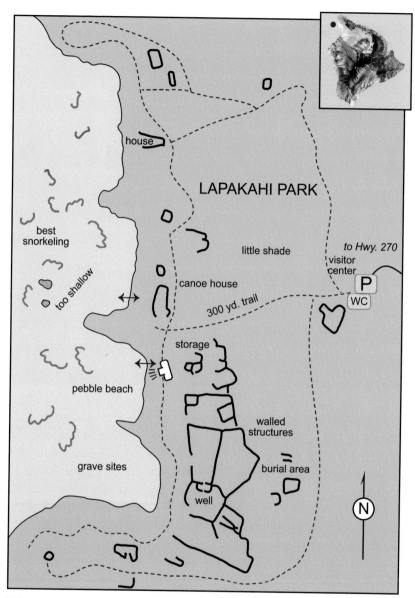

While the park is usually open from 8 till 4, it's best to call ahead if you plan to arrive on a holiday, when it might be closed. We've heard reports of snorkelers being turned away by the one and only park employee, so be prepared to accept an alternative (such as Māhukona) if this happens to you. We've even heard of people being told they couldn't sit. When a park is this remote and has only one person to interpret the rules, you might be stuck. We've never had any problem ourselves and recommend a respectful attitude to avoid any misunderstandings at this sensitive historical site.

Frog Rock

For a delightful and secluded snorkel, Frog Rock, north of Kawaihae Harbor, can be reached by hiking from a short gravel road off Highway 270. The water here is clear and the reef area extensive, so you'll want to stay and explore. Since there is no sand, only a boulder beach, access is easy only when seas are very calm. When swell rolls in (especially in the winter), Frog Rock can be downright dangerous. When off by yourselves, always snorkel in the morning before wind and swell increase by noon. Also, leave something bright on shore to help guide you back to the entry point. Follow our directions to this site, then snorkel along the coast in either direction, exploring the small coves full of interesting fish. This is a great place to watch for an octopus imitating the coral.

The peninsulas of reef extend far out to sea, so you can also follow them to see different creatures in the deeper water. The tops of some sections of reef come within about five feet of the surface, sloping down to about 30-50' deep. You may see divers out a ways, but are unlikely to see any snorkelers for miles.

This is one of our favorites for a long snorkel. Check out the arches, tunnels, tiny coves, and huge coral heads. Frog Rock has

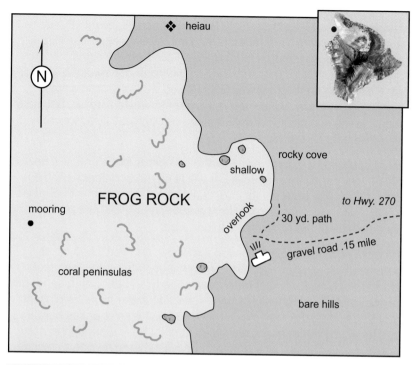

female psychedelic wrasse

some exceptionally pristine and beautiful coral. We once saw four octopuses here close together, a personal best.

Such a secluded site is usually for advanced snorkelers only, but beginners who don't mind deep water and have good swimming skills can enjoy Frog Rock on a very calm day. There are no facilities here, but nearby Kawaihae Harbor has restrooms toward the center and a simple shower and restrooms at the far north. Spencer Park, south of the harbor, also has full facilities.

GETTING THERE   Head north on Highway 19 (see area map, page 45) and take the Y to the left as it becomes Highway 270 (rather than right to Waimea). Following the signs toward Māhukona, watch for mile marker 5 to the north of Kawaihae Harbor. At .6 of a mile north of marker 5, you'll see a small public access parking lot and trail, which you don't want to waste time on, because it only leads to a cliff. Instead, continue on Highway 270 to exactly .9 of a mile past marker 5.

Here you'll find a gravel road toward the ocean, but a gate will now block your car. Only one small car will fit off the shoulder near the gate. Otherwise about eight cars can park on the ocean side further south (between Kohala Waterfront and the gate). Be sure that you park outside of the highway shoulder area.

Hike .18 of a mile straight toward the water, and you'll end up at a "lookout" spot where you can see the thirty-yard path down to a storm beach on your right (see map, page 57). Rather than sand, this beach is lined with chunks of lava. Enter the water from the closest rocks assuming the sea is calm. Please don't take chances here if you have any doubt about the swell. It must be low enough to allow a safe exit because there is no alternative exit and no one to rescue you. Water in this tiny cove is about 2-4 feet deep, so you will want to head out for more comfortable snorkeling.

The hill to the north of this site has a dramatic heiau that can be seen from land or sea, which will confirm that you've found the right spot. While there is more snorkeling along this section of North Kohala, the challenge is finding parking and safe entry. Frog Rock is one of the easiest and has excellent snorkeling. Well worth the effort.

(Note: proposed house development in this area may eliminate the access from the highway described above. If that happens, you'll have to come in by boat or kayak.)

Mel Malinowski

saddle wrasse

Passes

In order to comply with Hawai'ian state beach access law, resorts negotiate various systems to provide public parking for beaches. Some on the island of Hawai'i provide public parking lots with restrooms and showers, others have a more complicated pass system to limit the total number of visitors.

Currently the Mauna Kea and Four Seasons/Hualālai areas both use the pass system. You drive up to their guard stations and ask for a pass to public parking. Usually you'll need to specify which beach inside their resort. They will give you a pass to be displayed on the dashboard or handed over to another guard down the hill.

Each has a certain total number of passes and when they run out, you're out of luck. So come early (especially on a weekend or holiday) if you want to count on a particular beach. Late afternoons are usually available at most beaches.

All beaches in Hawai'i are public property, up to the mean high tide line, however, land access is often over private property. Large resorts must tolerate some visitor access. Blend in with the guests and you're likely to have no problems, but misbehave and you could be kicked out. Do treat the facilities and beach well because we don't want resorts to become any more restrictive than they already are.

After beach parking is closed for the night, you are always free to enter the hotel parking to dine or shop. Some will allow night snorkeling, but this is somewhat optional.

Even with a pass, be aware that the parking can be a long, hot hike from where you plan to snorkel, so check our maps to see where the nearest public parking is located.

NOTE: You always have the right to drive down to the public parking (with or without a pass) in order to drop off or pick up passengers.

South Kohala Area

In recent years, numerous large resorts have been built in the popular South Kohala area. They promote themselves as total destination resorts, and each has its own particular character. Some feel comfortably Hawai'ian; others seem more like theme parks just plopped down complete in a tropical setting. Construction continues as we write with huge numbers of houses and condos being added.

While many tourists focus on sunning, eating, water slides and golf, there are plenty of excellent reefs along this coast. There's an abundance of sun, little rain, and water conditions that are usually excellent in the morning most of the year. Swell and wind tend to pick up around noon and can be impressive, so get yourself out early if in doubt. Winds can sometimes abate just before sunset.

Many of the beaches front hotels provide very limited parking for the public, so the available parking goes fast. Guard stations limit the number of visitors to some of these beaches and you'll need to know the magic words that work with each.

South Kohala is an excellent snorkeling destination, perhaps even better for snorkeling than for swimming. The Mauna Kea beaches

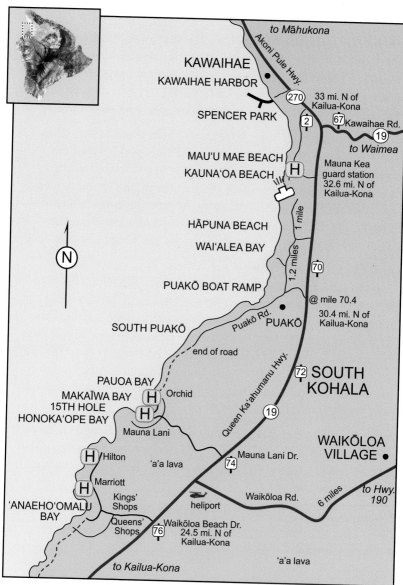

to Māhukona

Akoni Pule Hwy.

KAWAIHAE

KAWAIHAE HARBOR

270

33 mi. N of
Kailua-Kona

SPENCER PARK

2

67 Kawaihae Rd.

19

to Waimea

MAU'U MAE BEACH

KAUNA'OA BEACH

H

Mauna Kea
guard station
32.6 mi. N of
Kailua-Kona

1 mile

HĀPUNA BEACH

WAI'ALEA BAY

1.2 miles

70

PUAKŌ BOAT RAMP

@ mile 70.4

30.4 mi. N of
Kailua-Kona

Puakō Rd.

SOUTH PUAKŌ

PUAKŌ

end of road

72

**SOUTH
KOHALA**

PAUOA BAY

MAKAĪWA BAY

H Orchid

Queen Ka'ahumanu Hwy.

15TH HOLE

H

HONOKA'OPE BAY

19

Mauna Lani

**WAIKŌLOA
VILLAGE**

H Hilton

'a'a lava

Mauna Lani Dr.

74

H Marriott

Kings'
Shops

heliport

Waikōloa Rd.

6 miles

to Hwy.
190

**'ANAEHO'OMALU
BAY**

Queens'
Shops

76

Waikōloa Beach Dr.
24.5 mi. N of
Kailua-Kona

to Kailua-Kona

'a'a lava

N

Mel Malinowski

peacock flounder

61

are among the best for swimming on the island, with good snorkeling around the edges. The Mauna Lani Terrace fronts Makaīwa Bay, where you'll find the beginning of the Big Island's longest reef, extending northward past Puakō for miles. Picturesque Hāpuna Beach offers bigger waves for surfers and body boarders, while Wai'alea Beach offers a cozy, shaded and fairly protected beach.

While the winter will bring large swells from time to time, many of these South Kohala beaches are excellent a good part of the year. You will see periods of several days to a week in December through March where the swell and wind drop, the visibility clears, and snorkeling is crisp and dramatic. At times, a storm will come through, and there is no point in going into the water other than to bob around enjoying the swells, since you can't even see your feet.

On occasion, a fierce trade wind blows for days across the low center of the island straight for South Kohala. When this happens, you'll find better conditions either north or south. Kailua-Kona can be virtually windless while tourists in South Kohala stay indoors to avoid the wind. In very hot weather (especially September), you will appreciate the trade winds. When it's hot, muggy and rainy in Kailua-Kona, consider driving up to South Kohala. Since it sits in the rain shadow of Mauna Kea, and gets just a few inches of rain a year, bright blue skies are the norm.

Parking close to the sites is usually the biggest challenge, unless you are staying at one of the resorts. Some beaches have two public parking areas, so select the one closest to the best snorkeling area whenever you can.

Kauna'oa Beach at the Mauna Kea Resort and 'Anaeho'omalu Bay (in front of the Waikōloa-Marriott) are two of the more popular snorkeling sites in South Kohala. If you're looking for more seclusion, Wai'alea (with its shady beach trees) and Puakō (with a broad two-mile long reef) also have excellent snorkeling. Hāpuna Park offers a wide beach with great body-surfing, while Makaīwa Bay offers several small beaches with an extensive reef to explore. Kawaihae Harbor and Spencer Beach have some decent snorkeling and even better swimming.

All in all, South Kohala has enough variety to keep you snorkeling for a long, long time. That's why we choose to live here where we never get bored with our early morning snorkel on the "house reef."

62

Kawaihae Harbor

Kawaihae doesn't have the best reef around, but it is adequate and broad with easy entry and room to explore. A site to swim, snorkel or sun while others are busy fishing. You won't see lots of great coral or fish, but, we have seen mantas cruising the harbor. The area beyond the harbor is usually calm and only 10-15 feet deep for quite a ways out. Restrooms and a shower are available, but only a tiny bit of sand. There's very little shade on the jetty.

Due to increased security regulations, you can enter the main part of the harbor only once every three months. More than that and you must register, and take a class on security! Therefore, we now recommend snorkeling just beyond the canoe entrance (at the far north) rather than entering the main part of the harbor and snorkeling off the jetty. Enter the water from the tiny beach adjacent to the canoe entrance. It's a bit rocky, so the sea needs to be fairly calm. Snorkel to the right around the little point. The reef extends quite a ways out in both directions, so swim along the far edge for the best chance of seeing pelagic creatures such as manta rays. The fish aren't numerous, so Kawaihae isn't a first choice destination. Facilities include a shower, restrooms, picnic tables and plenty of parking with some shade at the north end.

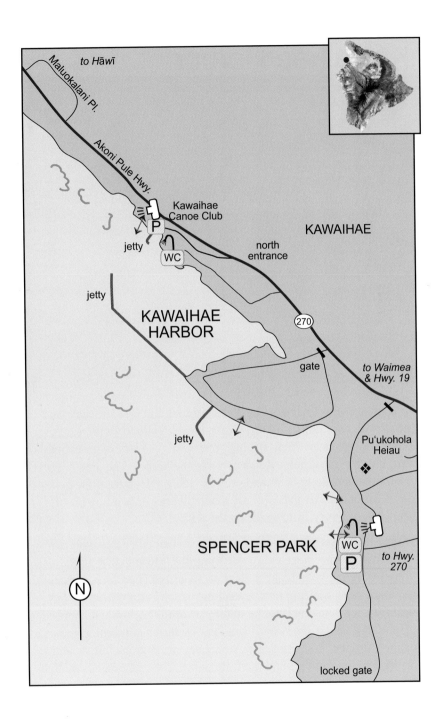

to Hāwī

Maluokalani Pl.

Akoni Pule Hwy.

Kawaihae
Canoe Club

P

jetty

WC

jetty

KAWAIHAE

north
entrance

KAWAIHAE
HARBOR

270

gate

to Waimea
& Hwy. 19

jetty

Pu'ukohola
Heiau

N

SPENCER PARK

WC

P

to Hwy.
270

locked gate

GETTING THERE From Kailua head north on Highway 19, heading left at the well-marked Y on Highway 270 (see map, page 61). Drive past the central entrance to the harbor. The next opening will take you to the canoe entry at the far right of the parking lot. Snorkel from the bit of sand just beyond the jetty that protects the canoe entrance. Continue to the right or straight out.

For the center of the harbor, you'll need to enter the harbor (with photo ID) and drive left, then right toward the middle. Snorkel anywhere along the outer jetty, going toward the sea. It's somewhat shallow (about ten to twenty feet) for quite a ways out.

Spencer Park

Spencer Park offers good facilities, fine swimming, but only fair snorkeling. The best snorkeling is located at the far left along the coast to the south and out to sea. There is also plenty of reef further out and to the right, although it requires a longer swim. The fish aren't abundant and the coral is scattered, but still you'll see quite a few of the usual reef inhabitants—ornate butterflyfish, saddle wrasse, lei triggerfish, trumpetfish, and sometimes an octopus or eel.

Watch carefully for big swell or a current off shore because you'll need calm water for safe snorkeling and won't want to get swept south away from the park.

In this elongated park, you'll find multiple restrooms, showers, picnic tables, camping, pavillion, shade trees and snacks. The sandy beach is a great place for a refreshing swim or for children to play and is somewhat protected much of the year. This is an excellent park to stop after a snorkel at a nearby site that lacks facilities.

If you snorkel about half a mile out and to the right, you will find a broad reef before the harbor breakwater. This isn't the best snorkeling around, but it's a good place to watch for pelagic fish—especially curious manta rays that often cruise this coast in ten to twenty feet of water.

GETTING THERE

Head north on Highway 19 and take the Y to the left as it becomes Highway 270 (rather than right to Waimea). Watch on the left for the sign just north of mile marker 2 (see map, page 61). Head for the parking area at the far left (south). Entry is easy from sand as long as the swell isn't high. Summer mornings are your best bet for calm conditions here. The reef isn't huge, but there's always something to see as you wander around the coral heads to the left and straight out to sea.

Mel Malinowski

male parrotfish

Mau'u Mae Beach

If the thirty beach parking passes for the Mauna Kea Beach (Kauna'oa Beach) are in use, consider asking at the same guard station for one of the ten passes to Mau'u Mae Beach.

Mau'u Mae Beach is similar to Kauna'oa, but smaller and less developed. With no hotel and no facilities yet, it also has few people, but plenty of fish and coral. There are plans for development at this site, so access will change. If it has, ask for directions at the guard station. For now, the gate for Mau'u Mae Beach closes at 5 p.m.

This is a picturesque, secluded beach with terrific snorkeling and swimming. Just snorkel along the rocks on the left as far as the point. It's calm, clear, and you might even have the whole beach to yourselves if you arrive a bit early. Bathing suits appear optional at this time. No restrooms or showers, but no crowds either. A delightful bay. You can always drive down to the Kauna'oa Beach path to use showers and restrooms after your swim. This requires another hike of about 250 yards.

Alternatively, for showers and restrooms, you can drive north to Spencer Park. You'll have to return to the highway because the gravel road is gated. Without the gate you could quickly drive north to Spencer Park.

GETTING THERE

Take Highway 19 north from Kailua-Kona to the Mauna Kea entrance (see area map, page 61). Turn left, then stop at the guard station (see map, page 69). Drive down the hill .4 of a mile, and take the third right turn (just before the road makes a sweeping 90° turn to the left). The third paved road gives the appearance of a hotel service entrance, and has a sign saying "Private Road". Not to worry! In .15 mile along this road, you'll see buildings and lots of service vehicles on your right just before the paving ends.

Continue on as the road becomes one lane, holding to the left through a chain link fence, onto the barely-paved road. Now you are out in the lava countryside. The road is narrow, but not difficult. Cross two small wood plank bridges and pass a private road on the left (see site map, page 69).

At 1/4 mile from where the slightly-paved road started, park along the road, remembering to display your beach pass on the dashboard. A small path on the left, near phone pole #22, leads through the shrubs toward the ocean. After about 125 yards, you'll come to a marker saying "Ala Kahaka", where you must turn left or right.

Take the left turn for another 125 yards through some small overhanging trees and you're there. (If you turn right at the T, you'll eventually come to a small rocky cove where a creek comes down— not the best snorkeling access, but a possibility if you just want a private spot to sun).

scrawled filefish

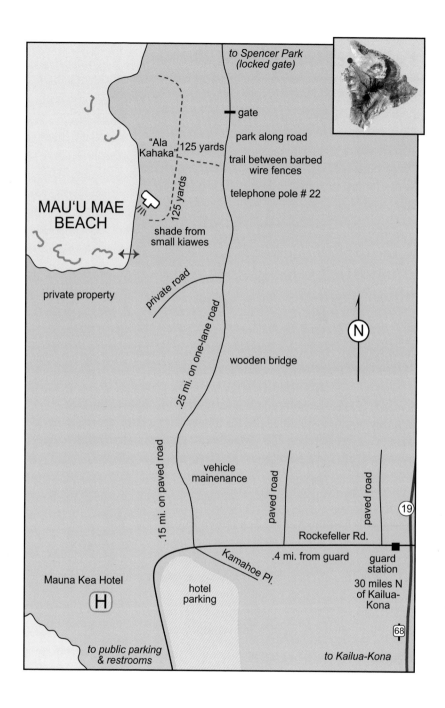

to Spencer Park
(locked gate)

gate

park along road

"Ala Kahaka" 125 yards

trail between barbed wire fences

telephone pole # 22

MAU'U MAE BEACH

125 yards

shade from small kiawes

private property

private road

.25 mi. on one-lane road

wooden bridge

N

.15 mi. on paved road

vehicle mainenance

paved road

paved road

19

Rockefeller Rd.

.4 mi. from guard

guard station

30 miles N of Kailua-Kona

Mauna Kea Hotel

H

hotel parking

Kamahoe Pl.

68

to public parking & restrooms

to Kailua-Kona

69

Kauna'oa Beach

In early 1960s, the barren 'a'a lava fields of Kohala seemed an unlikely and inhospitable spot for hotels. Though the area is fringed with beautiful beaches, they were hard to access unless approached by boat. Only local people visited these beautiful beaches.

This changed in 1965, when the first luxury hotel complex along the Kohala Coast was built on beautiful Kauna'oa Beach by L. Rockefeller: the Mauna Kea Beach Resort. This first hotel surrounded by 'a'a lava fields drew a rich and famous clientele for many years, and has spawned a host of other posh resorts. The beach chosen for this pioneer hotel remains one of the prettiest in Hawai'i, and is often voted best beach in the world. After a major earthquake in October of 2006, the Mauna Kea Hotel and golf course were closed for extensive repairs and remodeling.

Kauna'oa Beach has excellent snorkeling and swimming, and is an unforgettable day trip. A beautiful long crescent of soft white coral sand fringed with palms is set off by dark turquoise water. There is plenty of room for hotel guests and visitors alike. The water is usually safe and calm, but the hotel posts signs when warnings are in order—and often when they aren't. Many Hawai'an hotels post

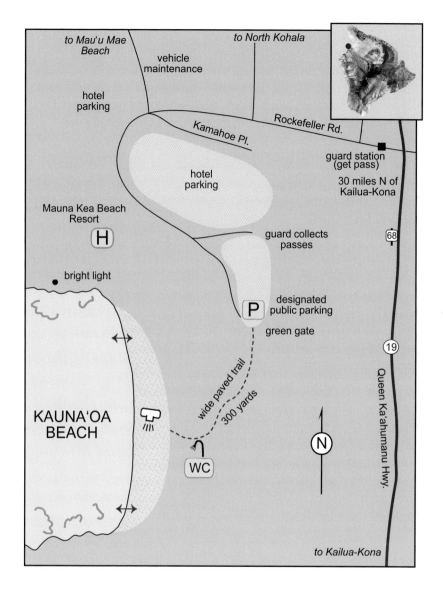

perpetual and extensive warnings for their own protection. Nearby we recently found a warning sign to stay out of the water due to a shark sighting, but it turned out to be a two-foot baby whitetip! Hardly a reason to close the beach, so we snorkeled on.

Snorkel either side out to the point—whichever appears calmest. The left has more coral, but the fish are plentiful on either side. We have seen turtles, eels, and a wide variety of reef fish. Choose the most protected side depending on swell direction.

This is a very protected bay with easy access from the sand. It can get a bit choppy far out at the points, but you don't have to swim that far. The excitement starts almost as soon as you enter the water. Come early in the day for calm water and an available parking pass. Roomy restrooms and showers are available near where the path meets the sand. Unfortunately, they have not been kept in good condition lately.

One word of caution. Small man-of-war or box jellies sometimes wash up here and can cause painful stings. We've known people who have been stung, but we have never encountered any here ourselves and we come often.

The Mauna Kea shines a bright light into the water in the evening to attract manta rays looking for a plankton meal. This is an outstanding place to snorkel with mantas when they show up. Bring your own dive lights. Snorkel on the north (right) side of the bay out no more than 100 yards to the bright hotel light. Of course, you'll need fairly calm water, but it often gets calm here in the early evening—especially in the summer.

Swimming with these 8-10' wide mantas is an unforgettable experience! In spite of the size of their mouths, they only eat plankton, not people. If you hit a night when the mantas don't show up, use your dive light to explore a bit along the rocks to spot a very different set of creatures than during the day. Watch for lobsters, unusual crabs and eels, and reef squid. Do be careful to swim around the shallow patch of coral near the beach, and approach the lighted area from the seaward, deep side to avoid scaping the shallow coral.

GETTING THERE
Go north on Highway 19 (see area map, page 61), past several major resorts, and on past the turnoff for Waikōloa. Continue past Hapuna Beach, to just past mile marker 69 (32.6 miles north of the Kailua-Kona junction). At the resort entrance,you'll see a guard station (see site map, page 71). Ask for a beach pass (see Passes, page 59).

With pass in hand, drive down the hill, curving left, on past the hotel and large parking lots. Enter the very last parking lot, where another guard will collect your pass. Drive on to the end of the lot, where you'll see marked beach access parking spaces. A wide paved path to the beach begins here. On your left, as you approach the sand, you'll find the building with public showers and restrooms.

Doctor My Eyes

If you are swimming along snorkeling peacefully and your vision suddenly gets blurry, don't be too quick to panic and call for a doctor. While you may have had a stroke or the water may be oily, there is a much more likely cause: You've just entered into an outdoor demonstration of the refractive qualities of mixtures of clear liquids of different densities. Is that perfectly clear?

Near the edge of some protected bays, clear spring water oozes smoothly out into the saltwater. As it is lighter than the mineral-laden saltwater, it tends to float in a layer near the surface for a time. When you swim into it, you'll often notice a sudden drop in the water temperature. The fresh spring water can be downright chilly.

Now, clear spring water is easy to see through, as is clear saltwater. If you mix them thoroughly, you have dilute saltwater, still clear. But when the two float side by side, the light going through them is bent and re-bent as it passes between them, and this blurs your vision. It's much like the blurring produced when hot, lighter air rises off black pavement, and produces wavy vision and mirage.

These lenses of clear water drift about, and often disappear as quickly as they appeared. Swimming away from the source of the spring water usually solves the problem. You can also surface dive down a couple of feet to see the effect disappear. Are you clear at last?

To see the mantas (at the north end of the beach), go at about 8 p.m. and tell the guard you're there to see mantas. Park in the hotel lot and walk through the pillars outside the hotel lobby. Continue about 100 yards until you see an orange elevator and take it to the G level. Walk out on to the beach, pass the shower, and head for the northern end of the beach. While snorkeling, stay seaward from the coral and lights. The brightly-lit manta area is less than 100 yards out along the north end of the beach.

If you do go at night to snorkel with the mantas, be discreet and respectful of the resort and its paying guests—access at night is a courtesy by the hotel, not a right like daytime beach access.

Hāpuna Beach Park

Hāpuna is a large, dazzling public beach, with restrooms, showers, snack shop, grass, lots of parking, shade, and covered picnic tables. It is open from 7 a.m. till 8 p.m. This is one of the Big Island's longest, prettiest white sand beaches (well, nearly white) and is very popular with local folks for picnics and fun. Swimming and snorkeling are both excellent when surf is low while surfing and body-surfing are great when it's higher. Hāpuna is one of the most dangerous beaches on the Big Island when the surf thunders—especially in the winter. Two lifeguard stations provide a chance to check with experts before entering the water. As Hāpuna has a reputation for having a short, hard shorebreak, ask before boogie-boarding or body-surfing.

The ocean can be calm as glass in the morning, then pick up quite suddenly around noon. For snorkelers who can't be watching the waves and fish at the same time, this can sneak up on you. During calm conditions, there is snorkeling at both ends of this long beach. Choose according to wave and wind direction. We prefer the north, where we can snorkel against the current, then catch an easy ride returning to the park. While the Hāpuna Prince Hotel fronts the far right (north) end of the beach, this whole long sandy beach is part of the Hāpuna Beach Park, and is available to all.

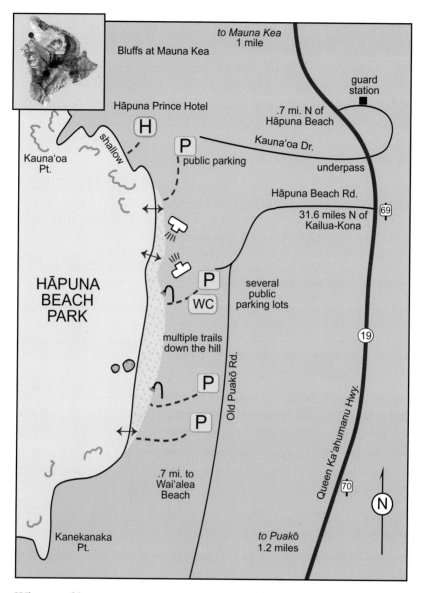

When surf is up at Hāpuna, try nearby Wai'alea or Kauna'oa for safer snorkeling. There is also a 3/4-mile scenic old Hawai'ian trail going north from Hāpuna. You may choose to enjoy the scenery and lively social scene here, rather than gamble with heavy waves—especially if you arrive in the winter.

On a calm day, this is an excellent choice for snorkeling, swimming, or boogieboarding. We have seen plenty of turtles, scrawled filefish, moray eels, rectangular triggerfish, yellow tangs, huge schools of black durgon, and nearly all of Hawai'i's butterflyfish amidst the healthy lobe and cauliflower coral.

Stay awhile and enjoy the park with its expanse of grass and sand. Plenty of lovely trees line the beach—including kiawe, beach heliotrope and false kamani. It is hard to exaggerate how pleasant Hāpuna is—it is one of our favorite well-developed beach parks in all Hawai'i. It is worth a visit just for a picnic if you're not in the mood for a swim, or the surf is up.

GETTING THERE

Go north on Highway 19 past several major resorts, and on past the turnoff for the town of Waikōloa. Soon you'll see a big sign for "Hāpuna Beach.", 31.6 miles north of the Kailua-Kona junction (see area map, page 61). This will take you directly to the center of the park, where you'll find plenty of parking, restrooms, snack shop, covered picnic tables, drinking water, and multiple paths down the hill to the sand (see map, page 75).

Park as far to the north as possible, because you'll need to hike north on the sand for the best snorkeling. Take any path down to the sand and head north on the sand to calm water for snorkeling. Parking can fill—especially on weekends and holidays, but is usually available if you come early.

Better yet for snorkeling, try the Hāpuna Prince Hotel exit, which will bring you to the public parking nearer the best snorkeling. Only about 35 spaces are available here and no facilities.

The Hāpuna Prince exit is easy to miss because the entrance is on the mauka (mountain) side of the highway. After you pass the Hāpuna Beach Park exit going north, look for the next exit to your right. Take this exit away from the ocean, then follow as it heads back under the highway. You'll need to ask the guard for a pass to park in the public access spaces about a mile from the guard station.

Pass the hotel and you'll see the bare public parking lot just before the road to the center of Hāpuna Beach Park. At the hotel's public lot, you'll be close to the great snorkeling, but not to any facilities. The beach access path begins at the far left corner of the lot. For showers and restrooms, you'll have to hike south along the beach or drive back to the highway and take the Hāpuna Beach turnoff.

Hapuna Beach south

Wai'alea Beach Park (69)

Tucked between Hāpuna and Puakō, Wai'alea (commonly called 69, after an old telephone pole formerly located there) is a lovely small oasis hidden beyond several private homes. Snorkeling is easy and excellent when the sea is calm. This bay offers far more protection from swell than nearby Hāpuna. A public park has recently been built and houses have been purchased for a pavillion area, so this is no longer an isolated spot with nude sunbathing.

Swimming is best to the right where there's a sandy bottom, but snorkeling is great in the center of the bay—in the area surrounding the small island. This is a chance to see pristine coral and plentiful fish, as well as turtles, all with only a short swim from a sandy beach. This is an excellent choice for either beginners or advanced. Don't miss this charming spot.

Stronger swimmers can check out the beautiful coral beyond the point to the right—a large area with plenty to explore when not too rough. In calm weather, we snorkel all the way to Hāpuna Beach.

The left also has an excellent reef that extends far beyond the point and wraps back toward the center of the bay. If you're planning to swim beyond the points, make sure that you go on a calm day. Early mornings are best. You'll definitely want to return.

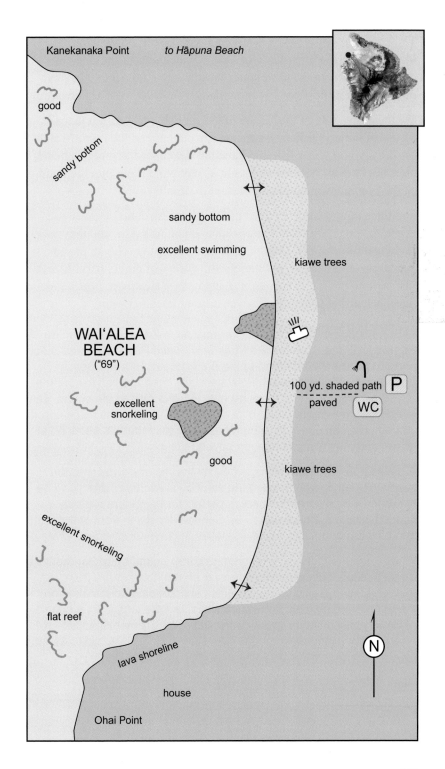

Kanekanaka Point   *to Hāpuna Beach*

good

sandy bottom

sandy bottom

excellent swimming

kiawe trees

WAI'ALEA
BEACH
("69")

excellent
snorkeling

good

100 yd. shaded path   P
paved   WC

kiawe trees

excellent snorkeling

flat reef

lava shoreline

house

Ohai Point

N

The beautiful sandy beach is covered with kukui, ironwood and kiawe trees providing plenty of shade. Watch out for those sharp one-inch thorns in the sand under these kiawes, however. They can easily pierce a flip-flop! Far more dangerous than most sea creatures.

We have seen lots of turtles, scrawled filefish, huge sailfin tangs, plenty of variety, and even a manta ray out beyond the point. Watch for the big porcupine fish that hang out near shore. Avoid this beach after heavy rains because suddenly a river will empty into the middle of the beach, bringing plenty of muddy runoff.

Facilities now include a paved parking lot, restrooms, shower and drinking water. Waiʻalea Park is open 7 a.m. to 8 p.m. and they no longer allow dogs, alcohol, fishing or camping. The 28 paved parking spaces can fill, but there's still plenty of gravel parking area just beyond the lot. If you want to enjoy Waiʻalea more like the old days, just arrive promptly at seven a.m. or late afternoon.

GETTING THERE

From Kailua-Kona, head north on Highway 19, then turn toward Puakō on Puakō Road (see area map, page 61). Take the first road to the right (toward Hapuna Beach). Drive half a mile (passing the private road), then turn left toward the paved parking lot. From here, it's only .15 of a mile to the ocean. The telephone pole where you turn is #71 (not #69). The lots holds about 28 cars, but can easily fill. No problem because there is enough flat gravel area for plenty of parking beyond the lot.

A paved 100-yard path leads by the restrooms and shower to the beach. Take this path through the scrubby kiawe trees and you'll be rewarded with a gorgeous beach, perfect for beginners and advanced alike (see map, page 79). Snorkel directly in front of the path and all around the little island.

When seas are calm, snorkel beyond either point. We prefer the left for snorkeling, but swimming is easier on the right, where there is a smooth sandy bottom. You can also snorkel beyond the sand on the right. Bring a picnic and stay a while, like the locals do. A couple of folding beach chairs and a cooler full of refreshments, and it's a beach party, island style.

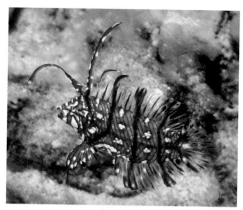

juvenile rockmover wrasse

adult rockmover wrasse

81

Puakō Boat Ramp

One of the Big Island's excellent but challenging snorkeling sites. Puakō Bay stretches along more than two miles of shallow, rocky shoreline. Since the waves can be high and the large inner lagoon very shallow out as far as 200 yards, this can make for a most dangerous entry and exit. Beginning snorkelers would be wise to snorkel here by boat only. There are certainly times when experienced snorkelers can find safe entry at both ends, but beginners should always be wary. Early mornings in the summer and fall will usually make for the safest and most enjoyable snorkeling. High tide or a rising tide is even better if you want to skim the reef. This is a huge area to explore, so allow plenty of time. Watch carefully for offshore currents, usually heading south. These currents are much stronger when waves are pounding the outer edge of the reef.

Experienced snorkelers can enter from the boat channel at the north end of the bay. Entry is easy as long as you don't slip on the algae that coats the edge of the ramp. We prefer to enter just to the right instead of using the ramp. Follow the boat channel out until the coral and clarity improve. Be alert for boat traffic, but it's light here and you may see no one in or over the water. When calm, this entry is fine for beginners who don't mind a long swim.

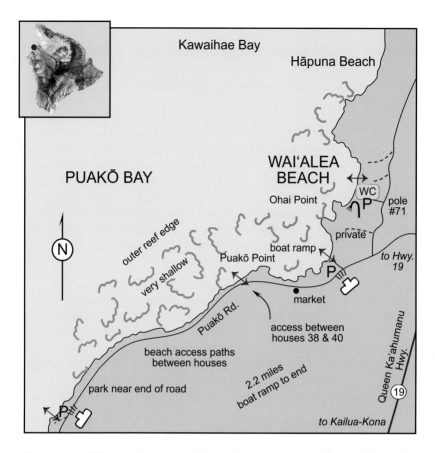

Tour around the reef to your right as far as the outer edge of the reef, taking care to avoid any area with surf. Noon brings wind chop and bigger swell, so come early to best enjoy this broad reef.

When conditions are calm, experienced snorkelers can also swim to the left and follow the edge of the reef as far as seems safe. Keep in mind the current tends to head south, so it could be more difficult to snorkel back against the current. You could drift snorkel all two miles to the end of Puakō Road, but it's a long hike back to the car.

The two-mile area along the edge of the reef offers some exciting snorkeling when calm. The reef drops off to fifteen to thirty feet, where we have seen turtles, eels, large pufferfish, schools of yellow tang, lots of healthy colorful coral and most of the usual butterflyfish: raccoon, oval, four-spot, ornate. Garden eels emerge from some deep patches of sand. You have a chance of sighting a reef shark and other pelagic fish where the water gets deeper off the edge of this large reef.

We highly recommend Puakō, but only for experienced and cautious snorkelers. Make sure that you never end up between large surf and this shallow reef. As long as you can stay beyond the drop-off, you will be fine. Swimming back in through the twenty-foot deep boat channel is also quite easy.

GETTING THERE

From Kailua-Kona, drive north on Highway 19 as it passes the big hotels near the Waikōloa. Continue north until you see the sign to Puakō and turn toward the ocean on Puakō Road (see area map, page 61). The road will turn back toward your left as it follows the coast south. There are six marked public access trails along this two-mile stretch. Some snorkelers take the access between houses #38 and #40. This nearly hidden path takes you to the middle of the reef, but shouldn't be considered by anyone without experience at Puakō.

The first public access at Puakō leads to the boat ramp (see site map, page 83), where you will find plenty of parking. Access is easy to the right of the ramp (ramps themselves are slippery). Follow the boat channel out at least 200 yards for the better coral. Then, meander over the reef to the right as long as you can avoid all breaking waves. There's plenty of good snorkeling along the far edge of the reef to the left, but check the current carefully before heading in this direction. Swimming north against the current can be difficult at times. This is more likely to be a problem when large waves are breaking against the long outer reef.

Mel Malinowski

saddleback butterflyfish

If You Love the Reef

- Show respect for the reef creatures by causing them no harm.

- Avoid touching or standing on the coral, as touching kills it.

- Come as a respectful visitor rather than as a predator.

- Leave the many beautiful creatures you find there in peace so that others may enjoy them as you have.

- Allow the fish their usual diet rather than feeding them. Feeding them ultimately destroys their natural balance, and causes their numbers to decline. It also makes them more aggressive towards people, and can result in fish bites.

- Global warming is gradually damaging reefs around the globe, so it's even more important to keep Hawai'ian reefs healthy. Do a part by minimizing spillage of any chemicals that may wind up draining onto the reef.

- Join our reef Easter egg hunt: try to find and dive for at least one piece of trash on every snorkel, and take it away with you. It sharpens your eye, and if enough folks do it, it will be hard to find any. Don't try to clean up the whole world. Just pick up one or two things every time you're out. This includes fishing line and sinkers.

- Use sunscreen less, and cover-ups more. Sunscreen dissolves in the water, and is toxic to fish and coral. A lycra body suit or a wetsuit takes care of most of your body anyway. For your sensitive face, wear a big hat. One of the best gifts you can give to the reef is to not pollute it with sunscreen.

multiband butterflyfish

85

Puakō Bay (south)

Although there are five public beach accesses (marked by small, sometimes hidden, signs) spread along the rest of the more than two miles of Puakō Road, all are risky because surf conditions can change suddenly and can trap you against a shallow reef. Very experienced snorkelers can head out from the public access path next to house #38, but only when absolutely sure about the conditions. We prefer to leave this entry to locals.

The safer southern entry is found near where Puakō Road dead-ends at the south. The south end of the reef is close to shore, angling out as it heads north. Instead of crossing the shallow reef, this entry allows you to skirt around the south end of the reef safely. Stay outside the shallow area and follow the edge of the reef as it heads northwest (to your right and out).

Keep in mind that the current here usually heads south, so head north and you'll have an easier swim back. Place a brightly-colored item on the shore to mark your entry because it's the only safe exit along here. Do NOT attempt to come in over the reef unless you have plenty of local experience. We have seen people stranded on top of the reef waiting for help while in a very vulnerable spot.

The Puakō reef is an excellent one with lots to see including garden eels (down about 30 feet), rays, most of the usual reef fish, and even a reef shark if you're lucky. Because of the sharp dropoff here, you are more likely to see pelagic (ocean-going) fish, such as bluefin trevally.

Come early in the morning (no later than 8 a.m.) for the best conditions. You're likely to have the whole reef to yourself before any boat excursions arrive. Wind chop and swell usually pick up late morning, but the afternoon winds often die out completely around 4-5 p.m., so you might catch Puakō calm before sunset. This is an excellent time to see the fish darting about, preparing for night.

GETTING THERE

From Kailua-Kona, drive north on Highway 19 as it passes the big hotels near the Waikoloa. Continue north until you see the sign for Puakō and turn toward the ocean (see map, page 61). The road will wind back toward your left as it follows the coast south. Look carefully if you want to see the six public access trails (mostly hidden between houses).

The first access heads to the Puakō boat ramp, then you'll pass short paths between houses. Continue 2.2 miles to the end of the road and park on the dirt just off the end of the road under the scubby kiawe trees. Look over the spots that allow access through the lava and pick the one that looks easiest. This is about 250 feet from the first car. The entry is often marked by little stacks of white coral on top of the lava, however, these can easily be moved. Chances are you'll see other snorkelers or divers entering from this popular spot.

It's helpful to leave something colorful to mark your entry because this is the best place for a safe exit—particularly if swell picks up, which often happens by noon. Do NOT attempt to swim in over the shallow reef. High tide makes this entrance even easier, although it isn't essential. If conditions are rough, don't even think of swimming or snorkeling from shore here.

No facilities are here except for one portapotty as you turn into the parking area. There's also little sand along this bay (mostly black lava and white coral chunks), just a wide shallow reef that's great for checking the tidepools, but dangerous for swimming. The deeper water beyond the reef has excellent snorkeling and swimming all along this broad bay. When calm, Puakō is a popular destination for excursions. Beginners might want to stick with excursions that access only the outer edge of the reef.

Pauoa Bay (The Orchid)

The popular hotel called the Fairmont Orchid at Mauna Lani has created an elegant tropical oasis surrounding the small, pretty white-sand beach on Pauoa Bay. This is an easy place to snorkel, but not well endowed with coral and fish. The rocky areas outside the inner bay are better for snorkeling than swimming, because of sharp rocks, coral and sometimes sea urchins in shallow water areas. Fresh water runoff is common here, giving an oily look to the water in places (see Doctor my Eyes, page 73).

Brown algae has covered some of the coral recently, although it can be somewhat seasonal. Still, there are fish to see such as the brightly-colored Picasso triggerfish—one of our favorites in Hawai'i. You'll find it in shallow water, not too far from shore. The Picassos prefer rubble and sand, so are not seen at all in the prettier coral reef further south. They will sometimes nip at snorkelers who get too close, but with very small mouths, they can't really do much damage.

The small bay is well-protected and not very deep, perfect for beginning snorkelers. More experienced snorkelers will prefer to swim much further out and toward the south. Or better yet, snorkel fabulous Makaīwa Bay south of the Mauna Lani Bay Hotel.

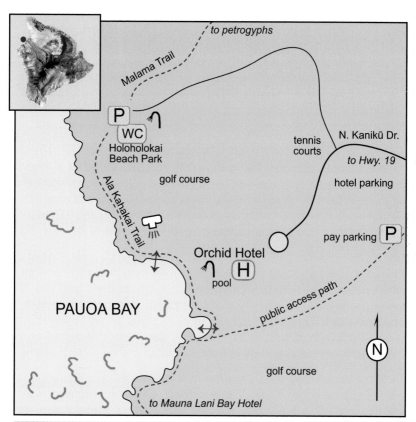

to petrogyphs

Malama Trail

P
WC
Holoholokai
Beach Park

golf course

tennis
courts

N. Kanikū Dr.

to Hwy. 19

hotel parking

Ala Kahakai Trail

Orchid Hotel

H
pool

pay parking
P

PAUOA BAY

public access path

golf course

to Mauna Lani Bay Hotel

N

humpback whale

Ray Lyons

89

GETTING THERE

The turnoff for The Fairmont Orchid at Mauna Lani is easy to find between mile 73 and 74 on Highway 19 (see area map, page 61). Three different public access paths are available within the large Mauna Lani property. Hotel guests can take a shuttle to any of the beaches, but public parking is less convenient. The three public parking lots are located at Holoholokai Park to the north, across from the small store near the center, and south near Honoka'ope Beach.

To snorkel at Pauoa Bay, follow the signs and park in the lot at Holoholokai Beach County Park, which is the next beach north along the coast road from the hotel (see site map, page 89). This will involve hiking south over some rough lava chunks. Alternately you can use the convenient Orchid Hotel parking lot, but it now costs $9.

After turning toward the Mauna Lani from Highway 19, bear right at the roundabout and take North Kanikū Drive, then take another right when you near The Orchid. This road has a sign and will lead you to the public park. It's a pretty spot for a picnic, with new showers and restrooms. The park also has plenty of grass, picnic tables and is an attractive spot for a picnic, however, the coast is lava shelf and rubble with no beach access in front.

To get to Pauoa Bay, take a quarter-mile hike south on a chunky lava path along the water. You'll quickly see why shoes are required—not just flip-flops. This is a sharp, 'a'a lava path with no shade! Follow the coast south, watching out for stray golf balls. As you near the hotel, choose a spot to enter the water. It's actually just as easy to enter the water at the alternative entry point shown on the map, across from the pool, rather than walking as far as the hotel swimming entry.

Snorkel out beyond the protected swimming cove. Visibility improves are you head away from the beach. When seas permit, snorkel across the broad reef to the south. Just be sure the offshore currents aren't too strong because those can carry you south and make your return difficult. Be sure to watch for the gorgeous Picasso triggerfish in the shallow water before you leave the little protected beach. And don't crowd them because they are fiercely protective and will occassionally bite—although with a very small mouth. These little beauties are probably the most aggressive reef fish in Hawai'i.

green sea turtle being cleaned by yellow tangs

Makaīwa Bay (Beach Club)

Less than half a mile south of the Mauna Lani Bay Hotel, you'll
find one of the Big Island's best snorkeling reefs. The area straight
in front of the hotel is mostly too shallow with too much swell for
safe crossing, but the reef to the south is just about perfect and is
protected nearly every day of the year. Snorkeling access is very
easy from the sandy beach, which has a nearby parking lot for resort
owners and guests. Public parking, however, is well-hidden and
requires about a 3/4-mile hike to the beach. The bay here tends to be
calm all day, but wind chop in the afternoon can reduce visibility.
Late afternoon sometimes brings calm again, although is rarely as
clear as morning.

Snorkel out here and you'll find a large horseshoe-shaped reef
stretching at least one hundred yards from shore. If you're staying at
the Mauna Lani Bay Hotel or the Terrace condos, it's an easy walk
meandering through the historic fish ponds and past the dive shop.

The reef here is excellent and uncrowded (except for middle of the
day and holidays). Beginners can find safe and easy snorkeling
near shore with entry from a calm, protected, sandy beach. More
experienced snorkelers will love cruising the whole area out to the
far edge of the reef and following it in either direction.

Snorkeling addicts will also enjoy heading to the left and around the
point (in calm conditions only, since this is more exposed to swell

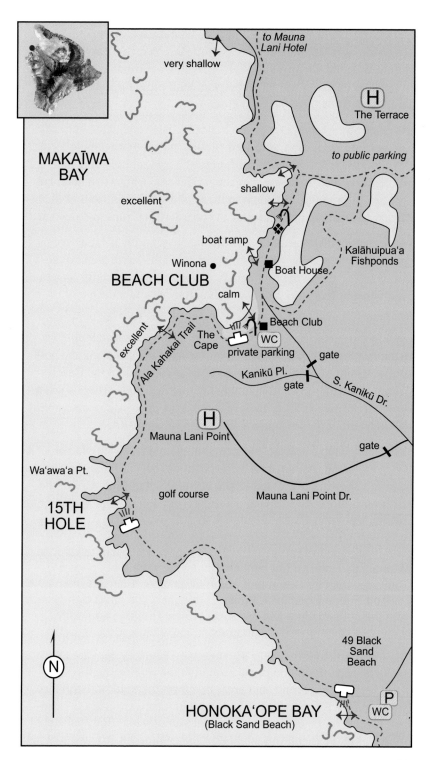

MAKAĪWA BAY

to Mauna Lani Hotel

very shallow

H The Terrace

to public parking

shallow

excellent

boat ramp

Kalāhuipua'a Fishponds

Winona

BEACH CLUB

Boat House

calm

excellent

Ala Kahakai Trail

The Cape

private parking

WC

Beach Club

gate

Kanikū Pl.

gate

S. Kanikū Dr.

H Mauna Lani Point

gate

Wa'awa'a Pt.

golf course

Mauna Lani Point Dr.

15TH HOLE

N

49 Black Sand Beach

P

WC

HONOKA'OPE BAY
(Black Sand Beach)

93

and current). Our favorite spot we call Grand Central, several coral peninsulas around to the left—easy to reach on a calm day, more strenuous when choppy. Just be aware of any current sweeping south before you head out too far. When the wind picks up suddenly, the swim back to the beach can be arduous.

We often see schools of raccoon butterfly fish, reticulated butterfly fish, spotted eagle rays, scrawled filefish, gangs of large blue trevally, peacock flounders, sailfin tangs, large schools of palani, and all the usual reef life. We never see the Picasso triggerfish here, but they are surprisingly abundant in the shallow water in front of the Mauna Lani Bay Hotel, out near the boarder float rope and beyond.

For a great one-way snorkel, follow the coast south as far as seems comfortable based on your swimming strength. There are several places to exit along the golf course. Poke between the little fingers of lava. Most of this stretch is about five to twenty feet deep.

A strong swimmer can go as far as Honoka'ope Bay, which is also open to the public. If you get tired of swimming, just scramble up to the Ala Kahakai Trail that's never far from the sea along the golf course. The trail is smooth enough to take you back to the Beach Club if you've brought along reef shoes or flip-flops. There's just a short patch (maybe thirty feet) of rough lava once you're on the trail. While barefoot is not impossible, it's not recommended.

The Beach Club restaurant is open 11 to 4, and has a simple but tasty cafe menu. A shower is available at the beach. Restrooms and a second shower are located on the outside of the south wall of the restaurant. More restrooms and a shower are found back at the public parking lot.

GETTING THERE
From Highway 19, turn toward the Mauna Lani Hotel on Mauna Lani Drive (see area map, page 61). Continue straight at the round-about for another 1.5 miles, then take a left on Pauoa Road for 1.1 mile. Turn right at the small sign across from the general store into the small (19-car) parking area with shower, restrooms and shade trees.

The trail starts to the right of the restrooms and wanders 3/4 of a mile through the Mauna Lani property (see map, page 93). You'll first cross a broad lava area, and then meander through the Kalāhuipua'a Fishponds. These historic ponds were used to raise fish, holding them within the traditional sluice gates. Baby fish could swim in, but as they grew, could no longer swim out. You will see fish

94

jumping in the ponds and quail walking on the path—a very lovely walk. When you get to the water, enter directly in front only if tide is high enough for clearance and the water is calm. Otherwise, continue walking left (south) to the sandy beach for the easiest entry. The hike from public parking to the beach is pretty and interesting, but a mostly unshaded 3/4 of a mile.

Even at low tide, the boat channel is also deep enough for easy entrance. Of course, the sandy beach entry is easiest of all. Snorkel out about 100 yards and continue to the right (north) to explore this excellent reef. You'll see a buoy for the Winona halfway to the outer edge of the reef. Depth varies from about five to twenty-five feet. Be alert for boat traffic when the sea is choppy because there are seldom many snorkelers out this far and you might be hard to see. Don't miss this excellent site. You'll want to come again because there's so much reef to explore.

Experienced snorkelers will enjoy swimming around the point to the left when swell is low. Follow the reef as far as you wish while making sure that you have the energy to return even if chop picks up, which it often does. On very calm days, snorkel into the spaces between rocks to check out the little unusual fish. This is the Inner Passage. Just watch out for those sharp black sea urchins.

If you'd like a detailed map of the whole property (with interesting narrative), stop at security on your way in (along the right side of Mauna Lani Drive) and ask for "View into the Past."

Don't forget to get your car out by the posted time since the parking lot will be chained off whether or not there are any cars still sitting there. We've seen tired, sunburned families trudge to their cars only to find the gate locked.

lei triggerfish

15th Hole

Directly in front of The Point condos, this entry provides an excellent spot for poking around in the shallows and between fingers of reef to see small creatures when the bay is calm. You can also stock up on golf balls while you're at it. Golfers have to shoot across the bay so they drop plenty in the ocean.

The best snorkeling entry is through a short wall by the large tree and a bench. You can enter from a tiny "beach" of well-rounded rocks— not the easiest walking, but better than lava. Leave a bag where you can see it from the water to mark the spot. You'll need quite calm seas to enter safely and wander in and around the many peninsulas that jut into the sea in both directions.

We see all the usual reef fish here as well as lots of small creatures. Try turning over a rock in the shallows. Sometimes every rock has a brittle star hiding underneath. A long snorkel to the right (north) will take you to the Beach Club, where you can walk back to the Point on a trail along the edge of the ocean.

No facilities up here near the golf course, but you can find showers and restrooms both at the Beach Club and the public parking lot. You'll sometimes see excursion boats anchor here, but if you come early (before 8) you will almost certainly have the whole area to yourselves. Enjoy!

GETTING THERE   If you're staying at the Point, you can park near building B, and walk out on the golf cart path to the 15th hole tee area, and head left.

Parking anywhere close is the problem here. If you're not staying at The Point or The Terrace condos, you'll probably have to park back in the Mauna Lani public parking off Pauoa Road, and hike 3/4 mile to the Beach Club. Then continue on the trail that heads around the point to the south. Follow it to the 15th hole of the golf course. Walk on the grass to the large tree with a bench underneath and a short wall with a gap near the bench. Enter the water directly in front and angle to the right a bit as you head out. Leave a bag so that you can return to the same spot for an easy exit.

An alternate, but rather long swim, can start at Honoka'ope (Black Sand) Beach (see page 93). This avoids the long hike, but you'll need to swim quite a ways across some fairly uninteresting sandy bottom.

female bird wrasse

male bird wrasse

Honoka'ope (Black Sand Beach)

This small blackish-sand beach now has good public access with restrooms and 20 parking spaces. No showers are available at the restrooms, but there is one down near the beach. We seldom see swimmers or snorkelers here unless an excursion happens to show up. Then it can become quite crowded—especially if they take over the small beach. Honoka'ope is also a popular kayak destination early in the day.

Honoka'ope Bay usually offers easy entry except for the small chunks of rock and coral as you step into the water. As you can see in the picture, there is lots of gravel in the break zone. Winter can take sand away and expose more of these shifting chunks.

Enter near the center of this small beach. Snorkel out beyond the point to the left when calm. You can snorkel to the right although will find mostly rubble near the beach. A VERY long snorkel to the right will eventually reach the Beach Club, opening out into

Makaīwa Bay, with plenty of excellent snorkeling along the way. Because of scattered coral heads, Honoka'ope is better for snorkeling than swimming. With a mask you can navigate around the coral. Watch for the bright blue encrusting coral that seems to thrive at this beach—at least it's unusually bright here. When it's choppy, stay on the outer edge of the reef. When it's calm, you can meander among the peninsulas of coral.

GETTING THERE

Head north on Highway 19 to the Mauna Lani sign (see area map, page 61). Heading toward the hotel, you'll come to a large roundabout. Go left here on South Kanikū Drive. Pass the King's Trail (the wide straight trail), then turn left on Honoka'ope Place. Stop at the guard house and ask for public access parking. Follow this road to the end (.7 of a mile) where you'll find a parking lot with restrooms. The hidden beach is only 100 yards away (see site map, page 93).

You won't be able to enter until the guard arrives, which seems to be somewhat variable. Getting in early can be impossible because the guard sometimes doesn't arrive before 7:30 or 8:00.

The guard also sometimes leaves early in the evening, which means you have to arrive a bit early for a sunset snorkel. Access is available from sunrise to sunset. The gate will always swing open when you depart, so you won't be trapped if you run a little late.

ornate butterflyfish

ʻAnaehoʻomalu Bay (north)

The northern edge of ʻAnaehoʻomalu Bay (in front of the Waikōloa Beach Marriott Hotel) offers good snorkeling if you don't mind swimming out past the poor visibility near shore. Head out from anywhere near the water sports shop. Entry is easy from the sand, but you won't see much near shore if swell has stirred up the sand. Swim out till the water gets clearer and the coral large and healthy. There is a wide area to explore on your right since the reef extends to the waves breaking against the far edge (somewhat in line with the two points). Avoid any areas of breaking surf. You should be able to find plenty of excellent, calm snorkeling. Water depth is good (5-20 feet) with large coral heads and plenty of fish.

We prefer to roam the area on the north close to the far edge of the reef. It's a long swim to the clear water, but much better snorkeling than the shallower areas near shore.

Showers are available near the water sports building, at the north end of the Marriott hotel. There is a hotel parking lot available up the hill with an easy walkway down to the beach. If it's full, you'll have to park about 500 yards to the north at the nearest public access. It's an even longer walk from the public parking south of the hotel.

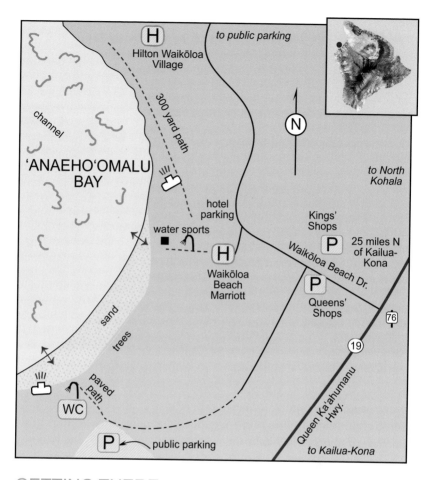

The map shows:
- Hilton Waikōloa Village (H)
- to public parking
- 300 yard path
- channel
- 'ANAEHO'OMALU BAY
- hotel parking
- water sports
- Waikōloa Beach Marriott (H)
- Kings' Shops
- Queens' Shops
- Waikōloa Beach Dr.
- 25 miles N of Kailua-Kona
- to North Kohala
- to Kailua-Kona
- Queen Ka'ahumanu Hwy.
- sand
- trees
- paved path
- WC
- P public parking
- 19, 76

GETTING THERE   From Highway 19, take the turnoff to the Waikōloa hotels (see area map, page 61). Head toward the hotels and follow the street as it curves to the right past the Marriott Hotel. Either park in the north hotel parking lot, or follow the coast north (staying left along the ocean) until the end where you see the tiny public parking lot next to the anchialine pool path to the ocean. Two public paths take you back to the bay. The first one that you'll pass near the end of the road has a sign: "dawn to dusk pathway" and crosses the ponds. Turn left at the path along the water and continue about 500 yards south to 'Anaeho'omalu Bay. Begin your snorkel in front of the water sports office near the water.

The other path leads toward the water from the northwest corner of the little public parking lot. It leads to the beach in about 1/4 of a mile. When the parking fills, you can still park along the road (for the time being anyway). The pretty eight-car parking lot is open from 8 a.m. till 8 p.m.

'Anaeho'omalu Bay (south)

The public park at 'Anaeho'omalu Bay (usually called "A-Bay")
is pretty, calm and very popular. Entry is very easy all along this
white sand beach and you can snorkel around scattered boulders and
some coral heads in five to ten-foot deep water. Because of the large
number of people and boats, the coral has taken a beating near shore.
The visibility is usually limited, due to the sandy bottom getting
stirred up.

The crowds and rather low visibility will put some folks off. Still,
most people like the wide and pretty beach with plenty of palms,
plumeria, and kiawe for shade. It's certainly a good place for children
and beginners, and there are just enough fish to make it interesting
for everyone. Snorkel anywhere among the scattered coral heads.

The parking area is gravel, with a short path leading to a lovely park
with showers, restrooms, attractive landscaping and a huge bay full
of boats, people, sports of all kinds, plus patchy coral and the usual
pretty reef fish.

GETTING THERE At the 76 mile marker on Highway 19 (see area map, page 61), take the turnoff toward the big resorts (including the Hilton Waikōloa Village). This intersection (Waikōloa Beach Drive) is 24.5 miles from the Kailua-Kona junction. You'll see the Kings' Shops on your right and the new Queens' Shops on your left. Turn left at the end of the Queens' Shops parking lot. Continue on through the open gate, curving right to reach the very last parking area near the water.

The 75-yard paved path emerges from the trees at the south end of 'Anaeho'omalu Bay. Restrooms and showers are available just in from the start of the path. This park is open 7 a.m. till 8 p.m., when the gates are locked for the night.

Mel Malinowski

eyestripe surgeonfish (palani)

North Kona Area

North Kona, with a large number of good (and often hidden) snorkeling sites, stretches from north of the Keāhole Airport to Kailua-Kona. There are a few very popular resorts (such as the Kona Coast Village and the Four Seasons/Hualālai), while home, golf and condo developments are fast covering what is left of the broad, bare black lava from Hualalai's last eruption, except for a few parks.

Here you'll find many a beautiful bay surrounded by white sand and palm trees where the 'a'a lava gives way to an oasis. The very bumpy road to Kekaha Kai Park (just north of the airport) offers access to three of these lovely bays. Excellent new parks have been opened at Manini'ōwali and Kikaua Point, where you will find soft white sand, turquoise water and all amenities—as well as public parking near the beach. Kīholo Bay requires a hot hike, but is beautiful and secluded, with fine snorkeling and swimming.

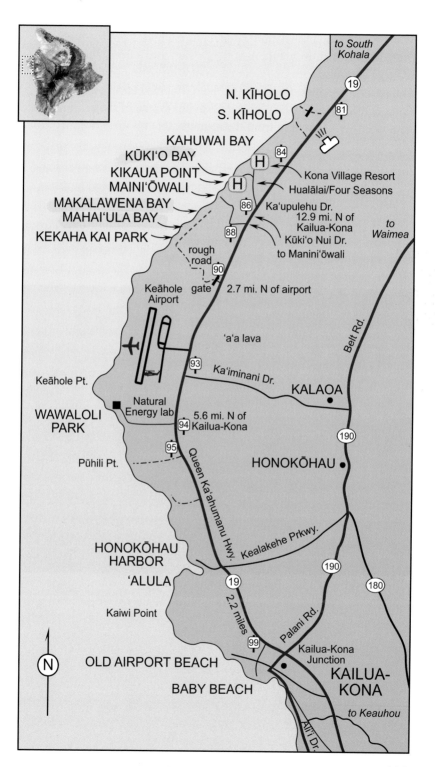

to South
Kohala

19

N. KĪHOLO
S. KĪHOLO

81

KAHUWAI BAY
KŪKIʻO BAY
KIKAUA POINT
MAINIʻŌWALI

84

H
H

Kona Village Resort
Hualālai/Four Seasons

MAKALAWENA BAY
MAHAIʻULA BAY

86

Kaʻupulehu Dr.
12.9 mi. N of
Kailua-Kona
Kūkiʻo Nui Dr.
to Maniniʻōwali

KEKAHA KAI PARK

88

rough
road

90

2.7 mi. N of airport

to
Waimea

Keāhole
Airport

gate

ʻaʻa lava

93

Kaʻiminani Dr.

KALAOA

Belt Rd.

Keāhole Pt.

Natural
Energy lab

94

5.6 mi. N of
Kailua-Kona

WAWALOLI
PARK

95

190

Pūhili Pt.

HONOKŌHAU

Queen Kaʻahumanu Hwy.

HONOKŌHAU
HARBOR

Kealakehe Prkwy.

190

ʻALULA

19

180

Kaiwi Point

2.2 miles

99

Palani Rd.

Kailua-Kona
Junction

N

OLD AIRPORT BEACH

BABY BEACH

KAILUA-
KONA

to Keauhou

Aliʻi Dr.

105

Many North Kona snorkeling sites require a hike from the highway, from a park, or from public parking located away from the beaches. We will continue with our counter-clockwise listing of the attractive and accessible snorkeling sites. In the northern section of the North Kona district, you'll find plenty of beaches (some of them large), but seldom easily accessible from the highway.

Kahuwai Bay, located away from public parking, and Kīholo Bay, completely secluded, both are well worth the hike. Makalawena and Mahaiʻula are two of Hawaiʻi's most gorgeous white sand beaches, so also worth the hike.

Smaller sites along the North Kona coast include ʻAlula Cove, Pāwai Bay, and South Kīholo Bay—all with easy access from parking and good snorkeling, but little in the way of amenities.

reef squid

Kīholo Bay (north)

This pretty oasis surrounding a shallow bay requires a mile-long hike from the highway or a 3/4-mile hike from the south, but is a delightful spot for a secluded picnic, swim or snorkel. The bay is mostly quite shallow (less than fifteen feet), and very calm. Snorkeling is decent, although not great, but the beauty of this bay is worth the hike. Fish here are mostly tiny (like a fish nursery), while the larger ones are skittish. Turtles seem entirely unafraid and we have seen as many as twenty of them. Beginners who prefer shallow water will really enjoy Kīholo Bay because it's only five to ten feet deep with easy entry from a sandy beach, although low tide might make it seem a bit too shallow for some.

This large bay is dramatic, with scenic views of the Kohala Mountains. You'll find a few empty houses, picnic table, and a 4WD road, but seldom any people in sight. This is a lovely area to explore, with reliably calm water for a quick dip or snorkel. There are no facilities here. For a distant glimpse of pretty Kīholo Bay, stop at the scenic vista along Highway 19 at mile marker 82 (see picture on page 104). Portapotties, but no shower, are located at the next beach to the south (see page 108).

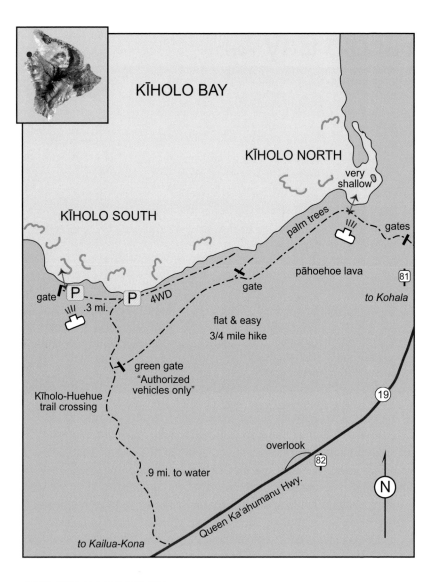

KĪHOLO BAY

KĪHOLO NORTH

very shallow

KĪHOLO SOUTH

palm trees

gates

gate

pāhoehoe lava

81

to Kohala

P .3 mi.

P

4WD

gate

flat & easy
3/4 mile hike

green gate
"Authorized
vehicles only"

Kīholo-Huehue
trail crossing

19

.9 mi. to water

overlook

82

to Kailua-Kona

Queen Ka'ahumanu Hwy.

N

GETTING THERE   For one hike, park along Highway 19 on either side of mile marker 81 (see area map, page 105). Pull off the shoulder onto the gravel area on the ocean side. Head toward the water and you'll find the path running toward your left (see site map, page 108). The path will wind back toward the water and continue for half a mile to the first gate. Then you'll need to hike another quarter mile to the second gate. At this point, walk around the closed gate, and head right about 200 yards to the water. You'll pass an old house on your left and a water tower to the right. The beach is mostly small pebbles, but the entry here is easy with calm water.

Most of the way you'll be hiking on an old 4WD road, however, cars can't enter due to the piles of fallen trees placed in the road to prevent access. This hike is about one mile long. Watch for green sand on the path. It's olivine left over from Hualalai's last eruption.

Another route is to drive down the gravel road at exactly mile 82.5 (just south of the Kīholo lookout along Highway 19. Follow the road .9 of a mile toward the water. Where it turns to the left, continue on straight ahead instead toward the water and park. Then hike a short way to the water. At that point hike a 4WD, loose gravel road north for about 400 yards to the south end of Kīholo Bay—passing a freshwater pool along the way on the right. This is a shorter hike with good parking, but the route is arduous, due to the loose gravel. Sturdy shoes are in order here. The last section of the hike is over chunks of lava and coral.

Probably the easiest hike is 3/4 of a mile along a gated gravel road that branches off the mile 82.5 road to the right at the locked green gate about .8 mile from the highway. As you near the shallow bay you'll find a shoreline access path on the left side of the road. This road is flat and easy compared to the trail closer to the ocean. We hike this route in only about 15-20 minutes.

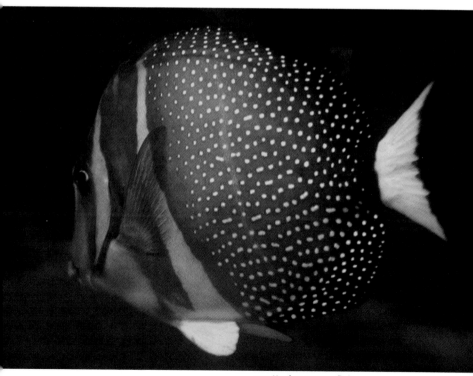

spotted surgeonfish

Kīholo (south)

This broad black sand and gravel beach has excellent access, but is used mostly by locals and not the most scenic in the area. Big waves make it dangerous at times, because the coral is all fairly shallow and near shore, but when calm it offers a fairly broad area of scattered coral and the usual reef fish. You might see people fishing, but seldom anyone in the water. The best snorkeling is to the left (south) and shallow enough to be popular with beginners. If there's a small shore break, just carry your fins as you zip through to calmer water, then put them on in the water. A good place to watch for that octopus. No facilities here except a portapotty, though there is plenty of shade. Watch out for those devilishly sharp kiawe thorns. Swimming is best at high tide, to avoid the shallow reef. When you see windsurfers, it's probably too choppy to snorkel.

When swell kicks up, you can always hike north to well-protected and shallow inner Kīholo Bay. Drive back to where the gravel road approaches the ocean, park here and hike 400 yards north on a loose gravel trail along the ocean (see map, page 108, with alternative hiking routes).

GETTING THERE

From Highway 19 (see area map, page 105), take the gravel road toward the ocean at exactly mile 82.5, which is south of the Kīholo lookout. The sign is placed just far enough away to be invisible from the highway. This is a one-lane public access road that should be open 7 a.m. to 7 p.m.. The moderately bumpy gravel road will curve to the left as you approach the water in .9 of a mile. Continue south .3 of a mile to where you can park anywhere near the portapotty and the abandoned octagonal house. The road is gated beyond this, so you can't go too far and miss it. When the swell isn't too high, walk south (to the left) and enter here, and continue swimming to the south to see lots of fish beyond the point until you're in front of the house with palm trees (once owned by Loretta Lynn).

While often nearly empty, this beach is hopping when windsurfers arrive. On holiday weekends, you may find wall-to-wall tents set up. Now that dogs are banned at most neighboring beach parks, you'll see more of them playing here.

Part of the reef here is close to shore, so enter carefully. The couple in our picture on page 110 are fine on this calm day, but with more swell they would need to cross quickly beyond the shallows. It often helps to carry fins and put them on after you reach adequate depth

Kahuwai Bay (Kona Village)

The elegantly-casual Kona Village Resort surrounds calm and lovely Kahuwai Bay, and the popular Four Seasons/Hualālai Resort is walking distance to the south. Snorkeling is excellent here when conditions are good—especially in the mornings. Finding public access is the hard part. We prefer to park to the south. Come early (before 8) and you may have the whole bay to yourself. Later in the day, the water tends to be choppy and you'll find more people, boats and kayaks. Late afternoon (4 or 5) often brings calm water again, but will be less clear with stirred-up sand from the day's activities.

Snorkeling is easy with entry anywhere along the broad sandy beach. To get to the far north side, either snorkel across the bay (plenty of clearance over the reef) or walk on the sand to the far northern end. There's plenty to see in the middle of the bay, but the best snorkeling is near the lava rocks along the northern end of the beach. When seas are extra calm, you can even continue past Mahewalu Point to find a tiny black-sand beach. Turtles are common at Kahuwai and manta rays sometimes feed in this bay. If you can get in at night, this is a good site for night snorkeling with a chance of swimming with a manta ray—always a huge thrill.

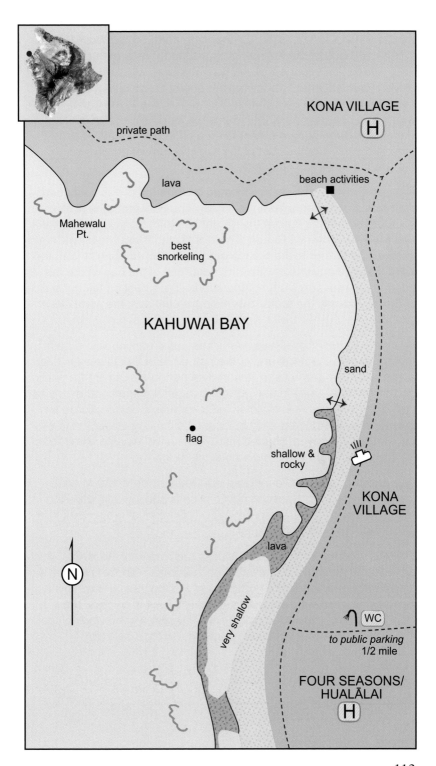

KONA VILLAGE
(H)

private path

lava

Mahewalu
Pt.

beach activities

best
snorkeling

KAHUWAI BAY

sand

flag

shallow &
rocky

KONA
VILLAGE

lava

(N)

very shallow

(WC)

to public parking
1/2 mile

FOUR SEASONS/
HUALĀLAI
(H)

GETTING THERE

Heading north on Highway 19, go 12.9 miles north of the Kailua-Kona Junction (see area map, page 105). When you see the Kekaha Kai Park sign, watch for the next exit on your left, then turn toward the ocean on Kaʻupulehu Drive and continue right at the next chance. Go .9 of a mile to the guard station, where you can get one of the 13 passes for public access parking. Park in the bare, square corner fenced off from the maintenance area and you'll see the start of the half-mile gravel public path outside the fence (on your left).

Restrooms and a shower are located on the right of this unshaded path about thirty yards from the ocean. The path emerges at the southern end of the bay on the border between Kona Coast Resorts and the Four Seasons Resort. There is lava in front, so you will need to hike a bit further to the right to get to an easy entry point from the sand. Explore anywhere within the outer half of the bay where the edge of the reef drops off, but the snorkeling is best on the north side of the bay toward the rocks. Swimming is best over the sand closer to shore.

While the Kona Village Resort itself has guest parking with a path much closer to the north end of the bay, none of that is available for public access. Kona Village Resort gets our no-star award for public access attitude—they make it as difficult, distant and unattractive as possible, presumably to maintain near-exclusive beach access for their guests. It would be easy to locate the parking closer to the water, and have a paved, shaded path. As it is, we imagine some folks go ahead and park in the main hotel lot.

Alternatively, for a prettier access path, our preference is to drive to the Hualālai/Four Seasons public access parking and walk north along the beach path (see page 113). This takes off from Hualālai's most northern public parking lot.

There is also a southern public access past the Four Seasons, which provides an attractive boardwalk beach access path that crosses a small bridge leading to the north end of shallow Kūkiʻo Bay. This end has difficult snorkeling access over shallow reef and rocks, but is a very pretty and uncrowded picnic spot. It's also a good wading spot for little kids. See our directions on page 116 for Kūkiʻo Bay.

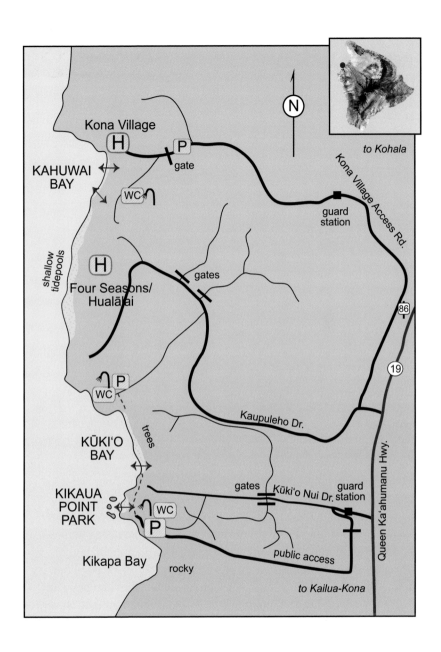

Kona Village

(H)

(P)
gate

KAHUWAI
BAY

WC

shallow
tidepools

(H)
Four Seasons/
Hualālai

gates

(N)

to Kohala

Kona Village Access Rd.

guard
station

86

19

WC (P)

trees

KŪKIʻO
BAY

Kaupuleho Dr.

KIKAUA
POINT
PARK

gates

WC

Kūkiʻo Nui Dr.

guard
station

(P)

Queen Kaʻahumanu Hwy.

Kikapa Bay

rocky

public access

to Kailua-Kona

115

Kūki'o Bay

— then walk to 4 Seasons Beach House for lunch.

You'll have to come early if you want to park at the Four Seasons/ Hualālai, due to the few public access parking spots. You'll need to ask at the gatehouse for visitor passes, then hang them in your car and park in one of the ten designated spots. The ocean here can be rough with lots of lava along the edge. The man-made lagoon provides easy snorkeling for guests only—perfect for a beginner. This is the kind of enhanced swimming pool we'd like to have at home—warm salt water, complete with lots of colorful fish. Several other small natural lagoons line the shore. All are too shallow for good snorkeling, but fun for little kids who wade. They might even get to see a fish or two.

The best snorkeling and swimming are found by hiking along the beach walkway to the north, where you can enter the water at Kahuwai Bay in front of the Kona Village Resort. Continue walking north on the sand to the far northern edge of the bay. On a hot day, swimming across the bay will be easier and more fun.

The public access south of the hotel is to the north end of Kūki'o Bay, which is a nice spot to picnic, but poor snorkeling and swimming due to the rocks and shallow water. We prefer to enter from the south end of the bay, but the north is OK when the tide is high. If you want to try from this end, enter at the far right of the beach, just to the right of our picture. This whole bay is somewhat shallow all the way to the points, so stay out when waves are breaking anywhere near shore.

There are about 40 parking spaces in this roomy, partly shaded lot with restrooms, shower and drinking water at the ocean end of the lot. The boardwalk meanders through a lovely area before emerging at a sand beach.

GETTING THERE   From Kailua-Kona, go north on Highway 19, then turn makai (toward the ocean) on Ka'upulehu Drive (see area map, page 105). This entrance will take you to the gate for the Four Seasons/Hualālai Resort (see map, page 115). To snorkel Kahuwai Bay, you'll need a pass to the small Four Seasons Resort public lot.

From here, go straight on the path (not right) for about 150 yards to a T. Go right at the T and you will come to a Y. Either direction will take you to the beach. At the beach, take the path along the coast to your right to find the snorkeling entries further north.

Beginners or children might want to practice their skills in the very shallow, enclosed pools in front of the Four Seasons/Hualālai Resort. Their deeper man-made snorkeling pool is reserved for guests only.

To access the north end of Kūki'o Bay, turn toward the ocean on Kūki'o Nui and get a pass for the Kikaua/ South Kūki'o public parking lot. You'll find plenty of parking as well as restrooms, shower and drinking water near this beach access. Kudos to the designer of this attractive, well-designed facility, a good example of how to mix private development and good public access.

It's possible to hike to the south end of Kūki'o Bay from the hotel, but easier to take a different exit from the highway (page 118). Drive to the parking lot and hike a bit past Kikaua Bay to the south end of Kūki'o Bay, where access to the snorkeling is easier (see picture of the south end of Kūki'o Bay, page 119). Enter from the beach right in front of the picture, where you can see a channel through the rocks. Snorkeling and swimming are only fair, and the reef is fairly shallow throughout the bay, but it's a lovely spot to picnic.

Kikaua Point Park

Public access to this park is now easy—as long as you come early enough to get one of the 27 passes. They fill early on weekends. The public parking lot is near Kikaua Point, where there is a beautiful protected, but very shallow cove—perfect for little children and picnics. We enjoyed a snorkel here early on a calm day when we could carefully skim the rocks and get up close to the fish. We even saw large schools of goatfish and convict tangs. All in about two feet of water, so take care to not harm the coral or yourself.

A short walk on the sand further to the north takes you to Kūki'o Beach, where you'll find a decent entry channel at the convenient south end. The rest of this broad beach to the north is too shallow and rocky for either swimming or snorkeling—especially at low tide. From the south entry you can snorkel way out to the orange buoy, where the shallow rocks drop off to about thirty feet. Because this whole bay is only about five feet deep, do not enter when waves roll in! Snorkeling is modest, but you may see some varied fish including the Picasso triggerfish, black durgons, butterflyfish, some huge unicornfish, morays and scattered coral.

Kikaua Point is a great spot to spend the day. Come early for one of the choice spots on grass under a big shade tree. Bring chairs and a picnic and enjoy the gorgeous view.

GETTING THERE

For the best snorkeling access to Kikaua Point and south Kūkiʻo Bay, head north on Highway 19 to the Kikaua Point Park exit (at mile 87) on Kūkiʻo Nui Dr. (see map, page 115). Drive straight to the guard for a pass, then double back to go to the south toward another gate. The guard will buzz you through after you press the button. This road will wind down to the public parking (over seven annoying speed bumps).

A wide concrete path heads out from the far end of the parking. You'll immediately see two very rough lava paths to the left, where there is a pretty bay with access only over rocks and lava. You'll probably prefer to keep on the concrete path. Walk about 300 yards from the parking lot and you'll come to the new restrooms, showers, and drinking water.

Kikaua Point is just beyond the facilities and has a beautiful fully-protected cove—perfect for little children. It is all VERY shallow (even more so at low tide), so poor for swimming. Snorkeling is possible, but kind of tricky to keep from scraping the rocks. If you're not claustrophobic, skim the whole cove and you will see quite a number of reef fish—with very close-up views. To snorkel here definitely come early on a weekday for clear water before people kick up the sand.

For more clearance walk across the sand to the next large bay to the north. There you can snorkel in five-foot deep water over most of the bay. The drop-off (to 30 feet) is way out near the orange buoy.

Manini'ōwali Beach

This gorgeous new beach park is at the far northern end of the
Kekaha Kai State Park land and has its own entrance. It does follow
the same hours (9 a.m. till 7 p.m.) and is also closed on Wednesdays.
Excellent showers, restrooms, and drinking water are available near
the end of the street, where you will find the paved walkway heading
down toward the beach, followed by a short rock/sand path.

Come early (right at 9), bring your own shade and stay for a great
beach to boogie-board, picnic, swim in the surf and catch lots of sun.
Snorkeling is only advised when the surf is low and is best at either
end—away from the sandy center. This beach is not well-protected
from open ocean swell, so is a good place to go when seeking waves.
When swell is low, there is excellent snorkeling at either end of the
beach and it's small enough that you can try both sides. Although
the fish aren't numerous, there is plenty of variety and even some
unusual sightings: Picasso triggerfish, turtles, spotted eagle ray
if you're lucky, lots of flounders on the sand, huge bluespined
unicornfish, unusual crabs, and more. Big winter waves can remove

much of the sand, so summer and fall are the best times to snorkel at this delightful beach.

The right side of the Manini'ōwali has a narrow peninsula extending quite far out and curving in a bit. The reef drops off to about thirty feet at the end. On the left side of the beach you'll find a broad rocky shelf with patches of coral and a good variety of fish in about five to ten feet of water. Often you'll need to make sure to stay beyond the breaking waves—especially where it's shallow.

GETTING THERE
Driving north from Kailua-Kona, pass the main Kekaha Kai entrance. Watch for mile 89, then turn toward the sea on the excellent two-lane paved road at about mile 88.5, where you will see the Manini'ōwali sign at the open gate, but not visible from the highway (see area map, page 105). Continue toward the small hill, curving to the right and ending up at the parking lot and facilities.

Take the paved path toward the sand, then hike down a short sand and rock path. When the parking lot fills on holiday weekends or any good weather day, there is parking further along the road, but you might have to drop off your gear, then drive back to park. If you stay to watch the sunset, keep in mind that the gate will be locked at 7 p.m. At least here there's a chance you'll be seen and reminded to leave before the closing.

Mel Malinowski

pinktail triggerfish

121

Makalawena Bay

This picturesque bay is secluded and surrounded by low sand dunes. While the snorkeling isn't the best in the area, the bay does tend to be much calmer than the main area of Kekaha Kai State Park (previously called Kona Coast State Park). It's a fairly long, hot hike over a rough 'a'a lava trail. The first part of the hike to Mahai'ula Bay is easy enough, but you'll find the path then gets worse (lava chunks the size of golf and even tennis balls) and very bare, so bring water, hat and cover-up if you plan to hike this far. Wear sturdy shoes too—this is not a flipflop trail. There are no facilities other than portapotties, but people love Makalawena Bay for its seclusion and gorgeous beach. Snorkeling is good and swimming is excellent, although you do have to watch out for some rocks. At Makalawena, you're likely to see turtles, but visibility isn't great due to all that lovely sand. Still, it's a gorgeous turquoise bay with fine, soft white sand and tiny secluded coves nestled between the low sand dunes.

GETTING THERE

Follow the instructions to Kekaha Kai State Park 2.7 miles north of the Keāhole Airport entrance (see area map, page 105). Park in the gravel lot on your left when you approach the beach (see map, page 127) and see a blocked-off 4WD gravel road crossing the entrance road. Hike on this 4WD road north. When you get to Mahai'ula Bay (there is an old building here), cut over to the beach side of the building. Take the unmarked path leading out between the building and the beach to the north. At first, you walk under a virtual tree tunnel of branches just past the building. Then you go on the makai (ocean) side of a water tower, where the path gets distinctly rougher and hotter. Hike another 45 minutes on this rougher lava. Wear hiking shoes if possible because there are stretches of very rough lava chunks. Don't do this in flip-flops. We've walked it in hiking sandals, but you risk cutting the sides of your feet on the sharp lava.

When you see sand dunes, watch for Makalawena Bay and pick your spot. Several trails cross over the dunes to the bay. You'll probably have a section of beach to yourselves. There are no facilities here except for picnic tables and portapotties. The hike is only about a mile from the parking area, but a slow and hot mile. Good hikers will find it no challenge, with a very nice reward at the end.

pufferfish

Mahaiʻula Bay

Nearly as pretty as Makalawena, Mahaiʻula Bay requires a much shorter and easier hike. It too has few visitors. This is a delightful little oasis with a coarse salt-and-pepper sand beach, shade trees, no facilities, but relatively calm water. While the snorkeling isn't exciting at this sandy beach, it's easy and you will see some fish and probably turtles. If you're very lucky, you might see manta rays because they sometimes spend time here.

This is an excellent swimming and sunning spot within easy hiking from the end of the road at Kekaha Kai State Park. Definitely worth the short hike. Mahaiʻula Bay seems more protected than either Makalawena or Kekaha Kai, so this is an excellent choice for beginners. And lovely enough to be worth the hike even for those who don't want to get in the water.

GETTING THERE   Follow the instructions to Kekaha Kai State Park 2.7 miles north of the Keāhole Airport entrance (see map, page 105). As you approach the beach, park early in the public lot on the left where a 4WD road crosses the entrance road.

Dive Boats

PADI and NAUI attempt to regulate the diving industry with strict rules, since there are serious risks involved. No one is allowed to dive without certification (backed up by a C Card). Anyone who wants to dive without proper training is certainly a fool, and the shops who will take such rash people out are equally foolish.

We have seen excursions all over the world offering to take people down without proof of certification. This is not the mark of the highest level of safety consciousness. Keep in mind that other advice and services from such operators may be similarly casual. Always take extra care with any rental equipment.

When their business is slow, some take divers (or snorkelers) to sites they can't handle. On the better snorkeling excursions, they keep a close eye on all their charges, so it's like having a lifeguard along.

Tagging along with a dive boat, you may find yourself on the surface as a snorkeler in much rougher conditions than the divers sixty feet beneath you. You'll need to rely on a buddy since the crew is usually more focused on the divers. It's a good idea to ask in advance whether good snorkeling is possible at the particular dive site they are planning for that day.

Most dive operators in Hawai'i run safe, well-organized excursions, and welcome snorkelers on appropriate dives. Don't be afraid to ask up front what their policies and attitudes are.

Park here and hike north on the blocked-off 4WD road (see map, page 127). Hike the old road 3/8 of a mile north until you come to multiple paths heading left to the pretty bay with an old house on the sand. This path is fairly smooth, but heads out across bare lava making it a hot trek in the summer. You may see wild white goats wending their way across the lava like mystical heat-induced hallucinations.

There are portapotties to the left of the trail and you'll see an old building as the trail approaches the bay. The south end of Mahai'ula Bay is reached from a trail that's only about 100 yards past the portapotties. There's plenty of seclusion available under the trees scattered around the low sand dunes.

Kekaha Kai State Park

Previously called Kona Coast State Park, the entrance to Kekaha Kai provides access to three lovely beaches. The long and VERY bumpy access road takes you slowly across the 'a'a moonscape to the main parking lot for Kakaha Kai, which is large, pretty and still fairly undeveloped. Sometimes the swell is quite high in the winter, but the reef is large and offers some protection when surf isn't too high.

Snorkel almost anywhere along the right half of the beach. There are plenty of coral ridges, so watch for clearance and incoming waves. You won't want to get caught between the coral and a wave.

Kekaha Kai Beach is large and we have had the whole place to ourselves—although fishermen arrive promptly at 9 on weekends. Some even hike in while the gate is still closed.

We particularly enjoy the sea turtles here. The water is often choppy and a bit murky, but still very interesting with plenty of good-sized pelagic fish. This is a popular spot for local fishing and you may

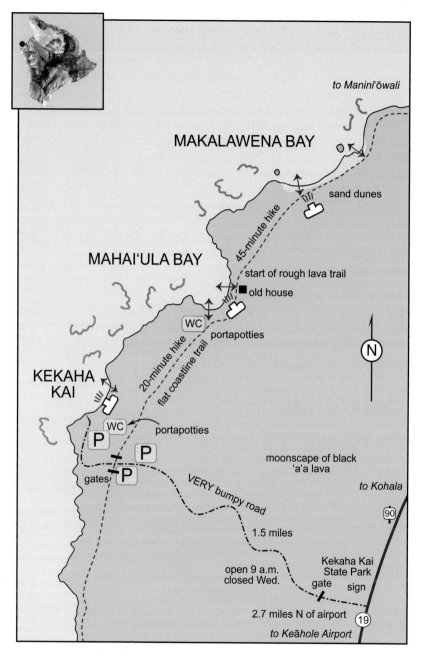

to Maniniʻōwali

MAKALAWENA BAY

sand dunes

45-minute hike

MAHAIʻULA BAY

start of rough lava trail

old house

WC

portapotties

20-minute hike

flat coastline trail

KEKAHA KAI

N

WC

portapotties

P

moonscape of black
ʻaʻa lava

to Kohala

P

gates

P

VERY bumpy road

90

1.5 miles

open 9 a.m.
closed Wed.

Kekaha Kai
State Park

gate   sign

2.7 miles N of airport   19

to Keāhole Airport

see someone who has caught an octopus. If the water here seems
too rough, consider hiking further to Mahaiʻula Bay or Makalawena
Bay, both of which offer more protection from swell and easier
swimming. Beginners should definitely hike at least to Mahaiʻula,
where the sea is calmer and safer.

GETTING THERE Take Highway 19 north 2.7 miles past the Keāhole Airport entrance (see area map, page 105). Watch for a small road to the left, 9.7 miles from the Kailua-Kona Junction. There is a sign, but it's easy to miss. Follow a 1.5-mile long rough road built across rugged and bare lava heading toward the ocean, over moon-like terrain (see site map, page 127). You may find the road too daunting, so don't bother if you hate lots of potholes. There are a couple of hills that are very close to 4WD, and can make some ordinary cars bottom out. Many rental cars and local sedans do make it through, so if you're a skilled driver, you should be OK. This is slow going at best. We really don't understand why the County does not pave this road, or grade it properly--perhaps it is meant to limit the access somewhat until there are more facilities? Don't show up on a Wednesday or before 9:00 a.m., because the gate will be locked and it is a very long hot hike. There is a bathroom near the parking lot, but no water or showers are available.

Kekaha Kai State Park has an excellent kayak entry point as you walk out on the sand to your right and watch for a good break in the reef. This is a popular spot to set off to explore the beautiful bays to the north. For kayaking, stay north of the old lifeguard station—now just a square of concrete in the sand.

Wawaloli Park

There are several beach access spots in this park, but none leads to safe snorkeling or swimming. The combination of rough waves and lava shoreline make it more suitable for surfers. It does have a shower, restrooms, and some trees, so you might want to stop here for the facilities. The reason for the big surf here is that the ocean floor drops off to about 2,000 feet right near the coast. This is a pretty and interesting place to visit even if you don't go in the water. Cold water from the deep is piped up to mix with warmer water, creating a thriving aquaculture business.

GETTING THERE Heading north on Highway 19 from the Kailua-Kona Junction, go 5.6 miles (see map, page 105). Then turn makai (toward the ocean) where you will find the Natural Energy Lab of Hawai'i. As you approach the water, a Y becomes a gravel road on your left leading to the good surfing. The right heads .3 of a mile to Wawaloli Beach Park, where you will find several beach access signs. The energy lab is located here because of the extremely steep drop-off, so the water is 2,000 feet deep close to shore. It is nearly always very rough here due to lack of protection.

128

Kaloko-Honokōhau Park

This pretty park down a gravel road offers picnic tables and restrooms, but no drinking water or showers. The park has a large fishpond and historic relics, so it is interesting, but not really a good snorkeling destination. The shore is entirely lava and the waves are usually large. The entrance road is also narrow and quite bumpy, so you may not want to drive here in a rental car.

If you go, check out one of Hawai'i's few protected wetland habitats and enjoy the tidepools, but stay away from the open ocean unless you hit extremely calm water conditions. Any entry will be over rough lava with the possibility of larger surf kicking up suddenly. This is a site best reached by boat.

GETTING THERE   The entrance is an easily-missed gravel road off Highway 19 (see area map, page 105). It is just south of Hina Lani (the Costco turn-off) and north of the Honokōhau Harbor (see map, page 131). Take the narrow, bumpy gravel road toward the ocean for .7 of a mile and park at the end. This is probably not the best road for rental cars. While the drive is arid, there is plenty of greenery when you arrive at this oasis of a park. Worth a stop, but not for a snorkel or swim.

Mel Malinowski

reticulated butterflyfish

Honokōhau Harbor

Just north of the harbor, you can head to the beach, where (with a short hike) you will find a pretty beach with a shallow, protected cove. High tide is essential for snorkeling and you'll want to swim out a bit for some clearance. This is a great spot for little kids to wade, but too shallow for good swimming. There are restrooms here with both restrooms and showers available back at the harbor.

GETTING THERE   From Highway 19, take the Honokōhau Harbor exit (see area map, page 105) at the light. This is called Kealakehe Parkway on the mountain side of the harbor and is 2.2 miles north of the Kailua-Kona Junction. After .3 of a mile toward the ocean, you will come to the harbor, where you should turn right. Drive through the harbor parking area, pass the restrooms, and continue to drive as far straight (west) as possible before parking. Ignore public access signs that will only make your hike longer.

From the end of the parking area, walk about 100 yards toward the water, then follow a sandy path that angles right for another 200 yards until you come to a T. At the T, turn left and you'll see the little sandy bay near the canoe shelter. Entry is from the far left because there's a bit more clearance on the left side. Snorkel wherever there is enough space. This isn't a good site for the claustrophobic. Fortunately, it tends to be very calm.

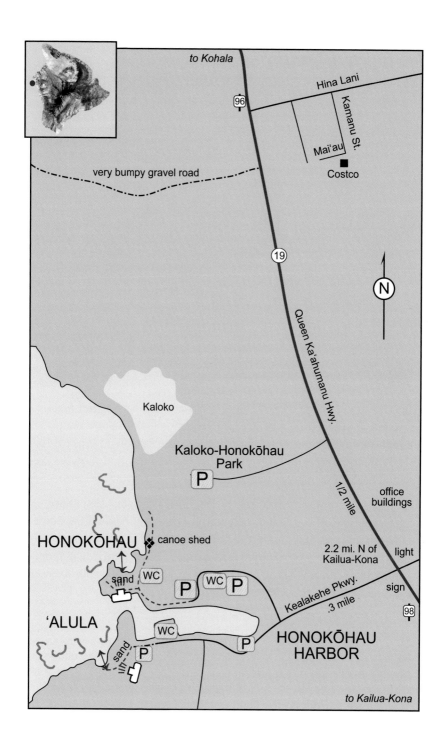

to Kohala

Hina Lani

96

19

Kamanu St.

Mai'au

Costco

very bumpy gravel road

N

Kaloko

Kaloko-Honokōhau
Park

P

1/2 mile

office
buildings

HONOKŌHAU

canoe shed

2.2 mi. N of
Kailua-Kona

light

WC

sand

P

WC

P

Kealakehe Pkwy.

sign

Queen Ka'ahumanu Hwy.

'ALULA

WC

.3 mile

98

sand

P

P

HONOKŌHAU
HARBOR

to Kailua-Kona

'Alula Cove

This tiny cove, called 'Alula Cove, is close to the harbor, but feels secluded. Its shape offers protection from swell and it's just deep enough for good snorkeling, but can be uncomfortable to cross at low tide. Although there are no facilities here, restrooms and showers are located back in the harbor parking lot.

Entry is easy from the sandy beach. Beginners can stay near shore, while experienced snorkelers will enjoy swimming beyond the point to the left and roaming out in the deeper water. This area is often calm enough to be an excursion destination. This is a nice safe spot to come with children since the beach is so gentle. Good spot for beginning snorkelers because it's calm and the swim is short, but most people will prefer high tide for the best clearance.

GETTING THERE
From Highway 19, take the Honoko- hau Harbor entrance (2.2 miles north of the Kailua-Kona Junction). Stay to the left side of the harbor (see site map, page 131). Pass the restrooms and shower to park at the western end where the road becomes sand. Park on the sand and you'll see the pretty cove to your left (.9 of a mile from the highway). Park and hike about 150 yards over lava and rocks to the small sandy beach. Snorkel straight out and around the point to the left when conditions are calm.

Mel Malinowski

Hawai'ian lionfish

Pāwai Bay (Old Kona Airport Beach)

Even in very small swell, this entry can be quite difficult because the rocks are slippery and there can be lots of spiny sea urchins. In fact, we once helped a tourist remove spines from her foot here. While the sea urchins move around, they tend to frequent just this sort of rocky, shallow bay. Low tide makes entry a challenge for beginners.

There are plenty of fish, but not much coral near shore. When the sea is calm, you can snorkel to the right around the point and along a rocky ledge, which is more interesting. Many snorkel and dive boats come to the deeper area regularly. Snorkeling from shore requires calm seas so that you can venture further out for the best snorkeling. Snorkel as far to the right as comfortable. Currents here tend to flow to the left (south).

This is a nice picnic spot and a popular local hangout, but there's plenty of room for all. If you always wanted to drive on an airport runway, here's your chance! Facilities include restrooms, showers, parking and picnic tables all back on the ocean side of the runway.

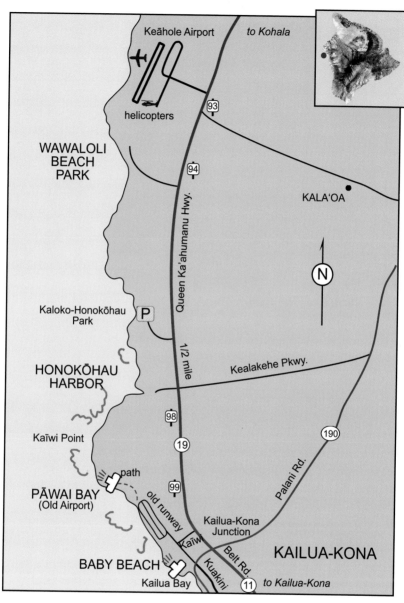

Keāhole Airport

to Kohala

helicopters

93

WAWALOLI
BEACH
PARK

94

KALAʻOA

N

Kaloko-Honokōhau
Park

P

HONOKŌHAU
HARBOR

Queen Kaʻahumanu Hwy.

1/2 mile

Kealakehe Pkwy.

Kaīwi Point

98

19

190

path

PĀWAI BAY
(Old Airport)

99

old runway

Kailua-Kona
Junction

Palani Rd.

KAILUA-KONA

BABY BEACH

Kailua Bay

Kaīwi

Kuakini

Belt Rd.

11

to Kailua-Kona

GETTING THERE

Take the Kuakini Highway north from Palani Road (the main drag in Kailua-Kona). This intersection is more or less the center of town. Follow Kuakini north. You'll pass playing fields on your left, jog a bit to the left, then the road eventually becomes an airport landing strip. Drive on the landing strip to the far end (at the north). Park here and walk out a short way to the end of the beach. It isn't far, but maybe best to wear shoes. Little shade is available on the path. Facilities are scattered makai of the runway.

135

Baby Beach

This small, but attractive beach is called Baby Beach because it's so well-protected and shallow. While it doesn't really provide snorkeling (well, a few fish) or swimming, we did want to mention the calm conditions in case you encounter rough water elsewhere. It's also a good place to teach little kids to snorkel. They're usually quite happy to spot rocks, little fish and people's feet.

Baby Beach is not easy to find and has no facilities, but offers a nice spot to picnic, cool off and meet toddlers. You'll find white sand, pretty small bays, two-foot deep water, and a protecting natural lava "breakwater" that stops the waves completely. Sand level will vary with the season, with more in the summer. A perfect spot for small children. Bring your all-terrain stroller, umbrella, water, hats and some favorite water toys.

GETTING THERE

From Highway 17 north of Kailua-Kona, take Makala Blvd. (at a light) toward the ocean (see map, page 135). Turn left on Kuakini Highway and watch for the Kona Community Aquatic Center on your right (just north of Kaīwi Street). Park in the back left of the swim center parking, then walk through the gate in the chain-link fence, between the soccer and baseball fields (about 100 yards). Angle left to another gate, where you will see public access signs. They will guide you down the steps, across the street, and to a 40-foot path to the little beach. From Kailua-Kona, just walk or drive north on Kuakini Highway, watching for the swim center on your left. The path is located quite near the intersection of Kaīwi and Kuakini.

For restrooms and showers, just head north on Kuakini Highway till it becomes the old airport runway. On the left (makai) you'll see many restrooms, showers, and picnic tables with shade.

More restrooms are located just to the north of the long stretch of playing fields. Scattered picnic tables are available there also.

male spotted toby

Kailua/Keauhou Area

This seven-mile long area within North Kona district contains most of the large condo developments and many of the hotels on the Big Island. Since so many tourists stay between the towns of Kailua and Keauhou, we've included it as a separate area.

Most of the coast here is rugged 'a'a lava, but there are numerous scattered small sand beaches. These beaches usually have considerably more sand in the summer. Winter storms take sand away and calm summer seas return it. Fresh water springs pour into the shallow bays along this coast, so you may be surprised to find cooler water in the most protected bays. The lack of sand actually makes for better and clearer snorkeling, although finding a safe entry and exit can be a challenge.

In Kailua, there are plenty of hotels, condos, timeshares, homes, restaurants and shopping. Kailua is the Big Island's most developed city. There are plenty of small coves scattered throughout the area and conditions are sometimes calmer here than most parts of the island. Kahalu'u Beach, with its breakwater, can even be calm during a big storm when nearly all other beaches on the island are too rough. There's lots of sun in Kailua, often rainy afternoons, and little wind, so it can be quite warm in the summer (especially September).

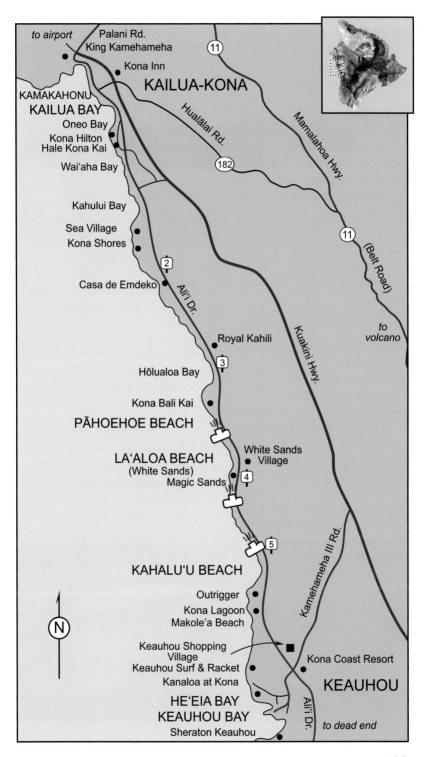

to airport

Palani Rd.
King Kamehameha

11

Kona Inn

KAILUA-KONA

KAMAKAHONU
KAILUA BAY

Oneo Bay

Kona Hilton
Hale Kona Kai

Wai'aha Bay

Hualālai Rd.

Mamalahoa Hwy.

182

Kahului Bay

Sea Village
Kona Shores

2

Casa de Emdeko

Ali'i Dr.

11

(Belt Road)

to
volcano

Royal Kahili

3

Kuakini Hwy.

Hōlualoa Bay

Kona Bali Kai

PĀHOEHOE BEACH

White Sands
Village

LA'ALOA BEACH
(White Sands)
Magic Sands

4

5

KAHALU'U BEACH

Kamehameha III Rd.

Outrigger

Kona Lagoon
Makole'a Beach

Keauhou Shopping
Village
Keauhou Surf & Racket
Kanaloa at Kona

Kona Coast Resort

KEAUHOU

N

HE'EIA BAY
KEAUHOU BAY

Ali'i Dr.

to dead end

Sheraton Keauhou

139

While people do snorkel directly off the rugged lava coast along Kailua, we recommend that most snorkelers stick with the easier beaches, in case conditions change quickly. Even a small swell can make your exit difficult where the lava is sharp.

Cool fresh water seeps into the bays along much of this coast, so don't be surprised to swim into some surprisingly cool patches. Water temperature will alternate as you swim. Fresh water will also affect the visibility by making the water blurry now and then. No problem—just swim a ways and it will clear up. Often you need to swim away from the beach to reach the warmer, clearer water.

When swell is low enough, there is usually some snorkeling within a mile or so of most hotels. All these sites are usable in calm swell conditions. Only Kahaluʻu Beach and Keauhou Bay have reliably calm water for beginners. Both beaches bordering the Kailua pier are the next most likely to have safe conditions. In-between beaches, like Laʻaloa and Pāhoehoe, are better suited to more experienced snorkelers and boogie-boarders.

Kahaluʻu Beach offers lots of BIG fish and comfortably shallow water. It's practically an aquarium full of large, magnificent fish that will let you come very close. Don't look for pristine coral here because years of tourist traffic have taken a heavy toll on the coral.

Keauhou Bay tends to be very murky near the sand, but has an excellent reef with good visibility further out in the bay, where the water is about twenty-feet deep. Few boats use the harbor and they always stay in the channel at the center, so snorkeling here can be quite safe when seas are fairly calm. We continue with sites listed in a counter-clockwise direction.

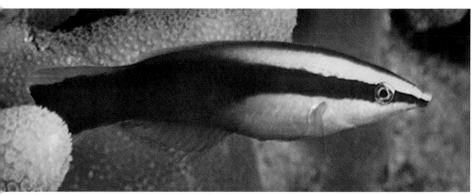

Hawaiʻian cleaner wrasse

Snorkel Gear Rentals

Should you rent, or buy? It really depends on your level of experience, and whether you expect to continue to snorkel regularly. If you're new to snorkeling, renting for a few times is a good idea, so you can try out various types of gear.

Gear rental is available in Hawai'i with shops scattered around the island, although not necessarily near your hotel. Snorkel Bob's and most dive shops rent gear. They advertise mask, snorkel, fins, etc. all for the low, low price of $9.95 per week, or $1 a day and such. This is just to get you in the shop, where they can sell you up to better quality, more expensive gear. We'd guess few people actually rent the bottom of the line stuff. Those who do probably later wish they hadn't. You're much more likely to pick the "dry" snorkel, comfortable mask, and prescription lenses. Expect to pay at least $30-40 for a week.

If you're really going to take up snorkeling or stay more than a week, and you have snorkeled before, perhaps you'd be better off buying your gear. You might want to check out more than one shop since most carry a limited selection. Snorkel Bob's even sells kid's packages with the agreement that you can trade it all in for partial credit when junior outgrows his. The larger size will run you half off if you trade in last year's gear.

The basic rubber fins are OK at first, but people tend to develop definite preferences over time. Leg strength will influence your choice and fit is always personal. If you do buy, make sure you can snorkel for at least an hour without getting blisters. Don't you just hate it when you buy a pair of $100 fins and then find they hurt your feet?

If you discover that your rental gear isn't fitting properly, take it back for an exchange or upgrade.

If you are near-sighted, a corrective mask is a must. Corrective lenses are available for anothing up to about 10 diopters. If you have unusual problems, such as astigmatism or quite unequal corrections, you'd have to have a special mask made in advance. Far-sighted folks benefit from a bifocal mask, which enables better up-close fish viewing, as well as watch or dive gauge reading. These cannot be rented.

Kamakahonu Beach

This little beach offers good and easy snorkeling. Parking is difficult to find here in the center of Kailua, but you might give it a try if you're staying nearby. Entry is easy from the sand in the usually-calm bay. To snorkel, stay on your right (west) and swim along the lava rocks as far as seems safe.

GETTING THERE   Follow directions for Kailua Pier (page 144). The hard part is finding a parking space—either in the pay lots or in one of the few free spaces on the streets. Walk toward the King Kamehameha Hotel (usually called King Kam). This narrow bay is found to the west of the pier, where you can enter the water without worrying about boat traffic. Snorkel to the right, but watch for rough water, and don't head into strong or breaking swell. Snorkeling is surprisingly good considering the crowded location. Stay very near the coast to avoid boat traffic.

Kailua Pier

Kailua-Kona is where the action is on the kona or leeward side of the Big Island—you'll go there to shop, to eat, or to hang out. This bustling town has grown up, or perhaps sprawled around a core of historical buildings that merit a visit during those odd hours when you're not snorkeling.

The Kailua harbor offers great protection and very easy entrance as long as you don't mind sharing the water with a few large boats. There's actually good snorkeling if you follow the pier, then continue up the coast to the northwest. The easiest entry is via the Kamakahonu Beach (see above), just west of the pier. If small waves are breaking onto the coast, it's still easy to stay beyond them.

The harbor area is often calm—something to remember on a stormy day. Use fins anyway because you may want to swim quite a long ways along the coast. This happens to be the site of the start of the Ironman Triathlon competition, so there's no room to snorkel when this popular event takes place. Watch carefully for boat traffic as you snorkel beyond the inner bay to your right along the lava shoreline.

Shopping and dining are available nearby, so there's plenty to do along several blocks on Ali'i Drive as it heads south.

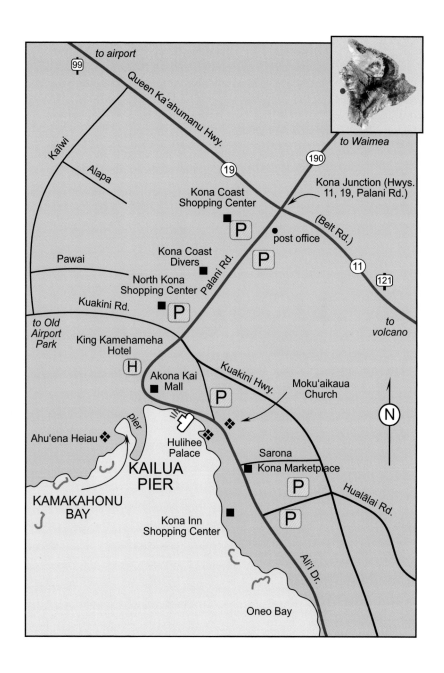

to airport

99

Queen Kaʻahumanu Hwy.

to Waimea

19

190

Kona Junction (Hwys.
11, 19, Palani Rd.)

Kaīwi

Alapa

Kona Coast
Shopping Center

P

(Belt Rd.)

post office

P

11

121

Pawai

Kona Coast
Divers

Palani Rd.

North Kona
Shopping Center

Kuakini Rd.

P

to Old
Airport
Park

to
volcano

King Kamehameha
Hotel

H

Kuakini Hwy.

Mokuʻaikaua
Church

N

Akona Kai
Mall

P

pier

Ahuʻena Heiau

Hulihee
Palace

Sarona

Kona Marketplace

P

KAILUA
PIER

Kona Inn
Shopping Center

P

Hualālai Rd.

KAMAKAHONU
BAY

Aliʻi Dr.

Oneo Bay

143

GETTING THERE

Take Highway 19 south past the airport, till you see the signs at Palani Road for Kailua (see map, page 143). Turn west at the Kailua-Kona Junction to drop down into town. As you pass the King Kamehameha Hotel on the right, and the road takes a 90° turn left, the pier is straight ahead. At this corner, Palani Road becomes Ali'i Drive.

Parking in town can look impossible, but if you keep trying, you can usually find space in one of the lots up the hill from Ali'i Drive.

Pāhoehoe Park

This long, narrow park, located on the beach side (makai) of Aliʻi Drive south of Kailua, takes its name from the smooth pāhoehoe lava. It's a good picnic spot with grass and lots of shade. Portapotties are located at the northern end.

Since there is more lava than sand, this isn't the safest entry for snorkeling—especially when waves are kicking up. Early mornings are the best time to catch calm conditions. Even then, Kahaluʻu, just a couple of miles south, is usually a better choice. When seas are very calm, you can snorkel all along this lava shoreline. Just be sure you aren't caught between a wave and that hard lava rock. It's better to stick with the sand entrance. While mornings are best, the sea sometimes gets very calm again in the late afternoon.

GETTING THERE   From Kailua-Kona, go south on Aliʻi Drive about three miles watching closely on your right (see area map, page 139). There's a sign near the center of the park and parking on the beach side of the road. If conditions aren't calm enough, continue south on Aliʻi Drive. The next beach (Laʻaloa/White Sands) is usually a bit calmer, while nearby Kahaluʻu Beach offers even better protection from swell.

La'aloa Beach (White Sands)

La'aloa Beach (also known as White Sands, Disappearing Sands, or Magic Sands Beach) is easy to find and convenient. It's a short walk from many condos and provides a nearby spot here for swimming or snorkeling if you don't have a car. While people do snorkel and swim straight off the lava rocks, this can lead to real trouble if the surf picks up. Leave such risky business to the most experienced local swimmers, and try Kahalu'u as your entry point instead unless the sea is unusually calm at La'aloa.

As these various names indicate, sand can vanish quickly in a winter storm. It can all disappear overnight, just like magic. When ample sand is in place, it's a pretty little beach, popular for swimming and body-surfing—especially for children. When the waves aren't too high, swim beyond them and snorkel this area toward the south along the rocks or north around the point. You don't have to go far to avoid the crowds. We've seen very few snorkelers here—often just a couple. Do stay out of the surf zone while snorkeling.

Facilities include a small parking area, lifeguard, shower, restrooms and picnic tables. Mornings and low tide are your best bet at White Sands. Often it's more of a body-surfing beach, but is pretty and worth a try. Snorkeling is best to the right along the lava shoreline, but currents and breaking waves can be a problem, so watch carefully and consult the lifeguard if in doubt.

GETTING THERE

Take Ali'i Drive south from Kailua-Kona about four miles from the King Kamehameha Hotel, where Palani Road becomes Ali'i Drive. You'll pass lots of condos and this is the first beach with facilities that you'll see. It's right along the road (see area map, page 139).

Mel Malinowski

spinner dolphin

Kahalu'u Beach Park

Kahalu'u Beach (sometimes called Children's Beach) is adjacent to the road, and clearly marked. It's small, but has ample parking, white sand, showers, restrooms, a covered picnic area, lifeguard and a protecting breakwater, creating a walk-in aquarium.

This is a good site for beginners because it's calm, has fairly easy entry (if you don't mind snorkeling around lots of legs) and an abundance of unusually large, gorgeous fish. It's all fairly shallow and the fish are often fed, so they are practically tame and can be seen up-close. This makes for excellent photo opportunities.

Please do not feed the fish because this disrupts the natural order, and ultimately leads to lower fish variety, as well as aggressive fish behavior. We're seeing greater than normal numbers of black durgons (somewhat of a weed fish) here—the more aggressive ones that crowd out other varieties of fish. Some large turtles also hang out here and seem able to tolerate the tourists.

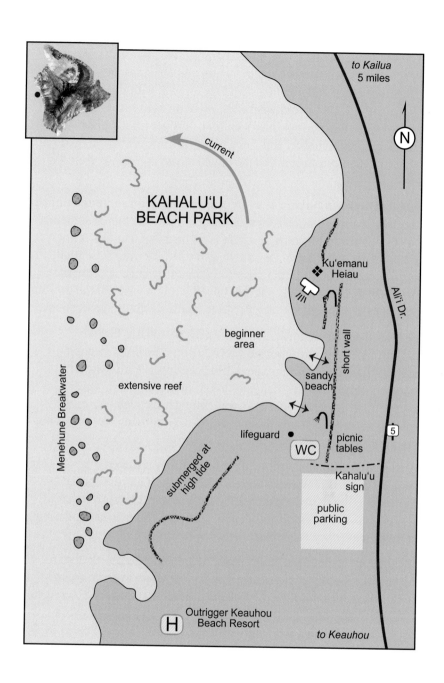

to Kailua
5 miles

N

current

KAHALU'U
BEACH PARK

Ku'emanu
Heiau

Ali'i Dr.

beginner
area

short wall

extensive reef

sandy
beach

Menehune Breakwater

5

lifeguard

WC

picnic
tables

submerged at
high tide

Kahalu'u
sign

public
parking

Outrigger Keauhou
Beach Resort

H

to Keauhou

149

The shallowness makes beginners comfortable, although crowds of snorkelers in a narrow, shallow entry can be unnerving—even dangerous (especially the ones who try to walk with their fins on). Come early or late, avoid weekends, or swim out beyond the crowds and this is a reliable snorkeler's delight. Just get off the plane, grab swimsuit, mask, snorkel and fins (even if it's late afternoon) and head for Kahalu'u Beach. It's the quickest way to recover from the long trip.

Some of you will be put off by the crowds, the fed fish, or the ruined reef tops from too much reef walking. Do your part by not standing on coral, or even touching it. There is no question that this is not a wilderness experience. Despite that, if you pick your time right, and you swim out a bit, the superb collection of large specimens of spectacular fish still makes this bay well worth a visit. Please do your best to help preserve this wonderful resource for future generations.

Besides the resident turtles, we have seen parrotfish, Picasso triggerfish, groups of scrawled filefish, Moorish idols, raccoon butterflyfish, Achilles tang, threadfin butterflyfish, blue-stripe snapper, ornate butterflyfish, pinktail triggerfish, yellow tang, trumpetfish, spotted trunkfish—well, you get the idea. We even spotted a rarely-seen tiny dragon wrasse flip-flopping along the sand, doing its best to look like a piece of seaweed.

A word of caution though: when the surf kicks up, even if it's stopped by the breakwater, there's still plenty of current caused by the water coming in over the partial breakwater. The current has a tendency to sweep north and then out, so stay closer to shore during storms and always wear fins.

If caught by the current, don't panic. It's much better to float out beyond the breaking waves and wait for help than to try to swim back across rocks or lava. At Kahalu'u Beach Park, at least, someone is likely to see you. Keep in mind that rip currents usually don't take you more than a few hundred feet (see Rip Currents, page 28 for more details). It's just a matter of all that water pouring in and needing somewhere to get out.

Early mornings and late afternoons are the best times to avoid the crowds. High tide provides a wider area with comfortable clearance. Low tide is OK, but you won't be able to explore all the interesting, shallow corners along the lava to the left.

Many island volunteers spend time here cleaning, painting and distributing literature to tourists. The "reef teachers" in blue T-shirts are available to take your questions about the sea life in this bay.

GETTING THERE   Take Aliʻi Drive south from Kailua-Kona (see area map, page 139) to the 5 mile mark (about a mile south of Laʻaloa Beach) and you can't miss this small park. See map, page 149 for the details of entry and where to snorkel. It's located immediately to the north of the Keauhou Resort. For the best fish viewing, swim just beyond the crowds.

undulated moray eel

He'eia Bay

He'eia Bay is also known as Walker Bay. You can snorkel here without worrying about boats or crowds. Entry is slightly tricky, since it's fairly shallow and more rocky than sandy. The bay is long and narrow, so it can be quite protected when the wave angle is favorable. Snorkel anywhere within the bay or beyond to nearby Keauhou Bay when weather permits. No facilities are available at He'eia Bay. There's a sand/gravel beach, but it's not the sandiest or the prettiest. Some seasons, the beach is all rock. This is an OK place for snorkeling, but not as good for swimming due to the rocks.

Narrow He'eia Bay is located just north of Keauhou Bay (an easy walk). It's tucked into a small residential area south of the Kanaloa development. There is public access from Manukai Street, although the path is somewhat hidden and overgrown.

GETTING THERE   If you happen to be staying near Kanaloa at Kona, He'eia Bay is just a short walk south. If you're driving, take King Kamehameha III Road from Highway 19 down the hill past Ali'i Drive (see area map, page 139), and turn right on Manukai Road. Watch on the left for a small street, then the path.

longnose butterflyfish

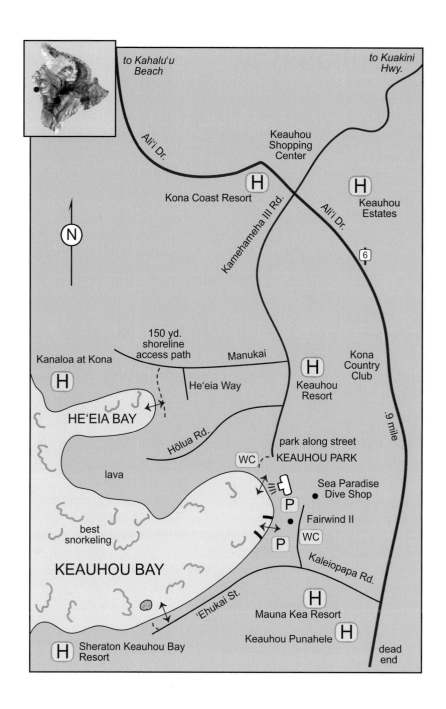

to Kahaluʻu Beach

to Kuakini Hwy.

Aliʻi Dr.

Keauhou Shopping Center

H Kona Coast Resort

H Keauhou Estates

Aliʻi Dr.

Kamehameha III Rd.

6

N

150 yd. shoreline access path

Kanaloa at Kona

H

Manukai

Heʻeia Way

Kona Country Club

H Keauhou Resort

HEʻEIA BAY

Hōlua Rd.

.9 mile

lava

park along street

WC KEAUHOU PARK

Sea Paradise Dive Shop

P

Fairwind II

best snorkeling

P WC

KEAUHOU BAY

Kaleiopapa Rd.

ʻEhukai St.

H Mauna Kea Resort

H Keauhou Punahele

H Sheraton Keauhou Bay Resort

dead end

Keauhou Bay

If you don't mind some boat traffic (although it's not frequent), this is an excellent place to snorkel and swim. There's a small park with a bit of sand, so enter along here. Choose whichever side of the bay is calmest. There's plenty of reef here, but stay inside the ample harbor away from any offshore currents and surf when stormy. Winter can sometimes bring big waves crashing spectacularly against the points, but the harbor itself is usually calm.

The Fair Wind and Sea Paradise offices are both located at Keauhou Harbor. The Fair Wind office is to the left of the pier, and the Sea Paradise office is on the right.

On the left side of the bay, the best snorkeling is out toward the point. There's plenty of good coral and fish here, so give it a try. You will need to swim a ways for the best snorkeling and clear water. We have seen lots of turtles, colorful Christmas wrasses, schools of raccoon butterflyfish, Moorish idols, pink and blue coral, but most after a fairly long swim. To shorten the swim a bit, you can always enter from the pier or boat ramp instead of the park area. All provide easy entry into the usually calm bay. A path near the island on the south side will place you closest to the best snorkeling, but not the very easiest entry.

The north side of Keauhou Bay is even better. Snorkel along the right side about as far as a line connecting the points, then head back to the middle of the bay (stopping before the boat channel). The first time we headed way out here, we were surprised at how much the visibility and quality of coral improved as we left the inner harbor. There is plenty of room to explore when swell isn't too high. Visibility is much better out here than you might expect when you first enter the water, where murky water usually cuts into your snorkeling enjoyment.

Keauhou Bay offers an excellent kayaking entry from either the park to the north or the boat ramp to the south. When seas are calm, you can kayak out of the bay and along the Kona coast in either direction—stopping to snorkel off the lava coast.

Manta rays like to gather at night in the 20-foot deep water off the southern point, where the hotel used to shine bright lights to attract them. The hotel (reopened as the Sheraton Keauhou Bay Resort and Spa) may do the same in the future. If so, it's possible to swim out here on a very calm night. The major hazard here at night is from dive boats, so you would definitely need strong lights to be easily seen. Advanced snorkelers only at night here.

GETTING THERE

For the easiest route to snorkeling, take the King Kamehameha III (called "Kam III") Highway exit from Highway 11 in Keauhou. Follow Kam III to the very end and park along the side of the road. Follow the short path or driveway to the park and facilities (see area map, page 139).

To drive to the harbor from the corner of Ali'i Drive and Kamehameha III Road, go .9 mile south on Ali'i Drive. Turn right on Kaleiopapa Street at the "dead end" sign (see site map, page 153). Drive on to the "Keauhou Pier" sign. Park outside the tiny congested pier parking lot if you don't want to get stuck in a mini traffic jam. It's a short walk from the bigger parking lot. There is another lot for Fair Wind and Sea Paradise customers just up the street.

South Kona Area

The Big Island takes on a greener, cooler look as you head south of Keauhou through the South Kona district. These steeper, better watered hills of South Kona are ideal for growing coffee, macadamia nuts, and tropical flowers. The bays are large and offer some excellent snorkeling in beautiful settings.

Although there are no big hotels as we write, two huge and controversial luxury golf, homesite and condo developments are under construction just north of Kealakekua Bay. A third development that would reach close to the Monument appears to have been blocked, due to strong community opposition. Runoff from the golf courses and streets could gradually damage extraordinary and pristine Kealakeakua Bay. We hope that this irreplaceable bay is not ruined by overly permissive development.

Two large bays in South Kona offer some of the best snorkeling in all the major Hawai'ian islands. Kealakekua Bay and Hōnaunau Bay are

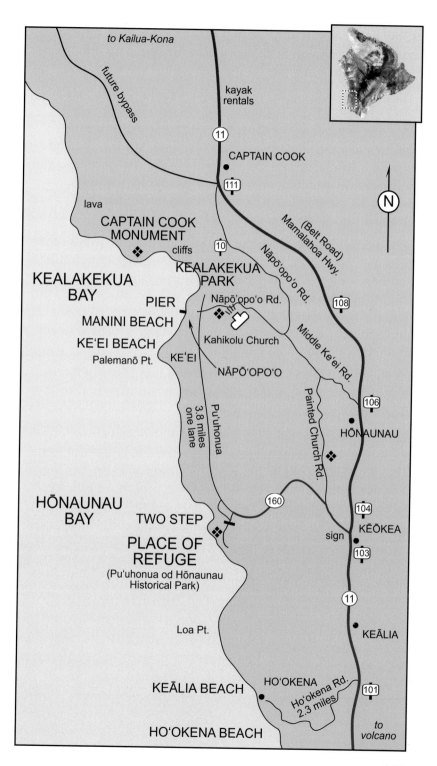

to Kailua-Kona

future bypass

kayak rentals

11

CAPTAIN COOK

111

(Belt Road)
Mamalahoa Hwy.

lava

CAPTAIN COOK
MONUMENT

cliffs

10

Nāpōʻopoʻo Rd.

KEALAKEKUA
PARK

108

KEALAKEKUA
BAY

PIER

Nāpōʻopoʻo Rd.

MANINI BEACH

Middle Keʻei Rd.

KEʻEI BEACH

Kahikolu Church

Palemanō Pt.

KEʻEI

NĀPŌʻOPOʻO

106

3.8 miles
one lane

Puʻuhonua

Painted Church Rd.

HŌNAUNAU

HŌNAUNAU
BAY

TWO STEP

160

104

PLACE OF
REFUGE

KĒŌKEA

sign

103

(Puʻuhonua od Hōnaunau
Historical Park)

11

Loa Pt.

KEĀLIA

KEĀLIA BEACH

HOʻOKENA

Hoʻokena Rd.
2.3 miles

101

HOʻOKENA BEACH

to volcano

N

both high on our list of snorkeling sites. They are large, usually calm, and have extensive reefs for exploration. Be sure to try both—unless you get very unlucky with the weather.

The Captain Cook monument in Kealakekua Bay is nearly always calm, but difficult to reach unless you take an excursion from Keauhou or kayak across the mile-wide bay. Strong swimmers can cross the bay, while sturdy hikers can make it down from the highway. Snorkeling near the monument in about ten feet of water is delightful—especially with the deep indigo of the bay right nearby. It's a chance to see plenty of reef fish near shore and pelagic creatures beyond the edge of the reef.

Increasingly popular Hōnaunau Bay is easier to reach, with an entry from the smooth lava. You can also walk through the historical park and enter via a protected little bay where canoes were launched. Hōnaunau Bay has reef throughout with varied depths, canyons and arches. Explore any direction within the protected bay to view a large variety of sea life. Beginners can stay near shore where the water is about ten feet deep.

Puʻuhonua o Hōnaunau National Historical Park (Place of Refuge) is an enchanting park, which shouldn't be missed with or without a snorkeling break.

Keʻei, Hoʻokena and Miloliʻi Bays (all further south) also offer good snorkeling, but are considerably less protected and out of the way. They are more exposed to swell across shallow reefs, so they should only be attempted by experienced snorkelers. We begin with the very famous Kealakekua Bay, where Captain Cook met his end.

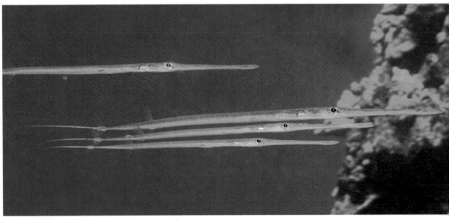

cornetfish

Kealakeakua Bay

Beautiful Kealakekua Bay is about one mile wide, extending from the Captain Cook Monument on the north, to the former fishing community of Nāpōʻopoʻo in the south. It's usually quite calm and offers some of the best snorkeling in the Hawaiʻian islands.

The bay tends to be unusually calm even in winter. With good fins it's possible to swim the one mile across the bay (even less if you walk to the far end of the beach). To swim here, you'll need to cross the deep center of the bay or follow the cliffs from Nāpōʻopoʻo. This is a long swim, so you need to either be in good shape or allow plenty of time to rest along the way. Fins are essential and a wet suit makes it easier to stay as long as you like without getting chilled.

The middle of the bay is deep, without coral, but often has as many as 200 spinner dolphins playing around in small groups, or pods. It's quite a thrill to watch them swim under you and jump out of the water—sometimes spinning in the air! Watch, but don't disturb them.

The best snorkeling in Kealakekua Bay is found in the clear waters near the Captain Cook Monument, where you'll find coral, eels, turkeyfish, Potter's angelfish, and an endless variety of other colorful fish. Very late afternoon might not be the best time to try this swim. The sea is often rougher then, and sharks are reputed to come in to feed as night approaches. We've only seen baby sharks here, and even then very rarely, though we often snorkel until sundown.

It's also possible to see this area by kayak, which can be rented in several shops up along the highway. If you do rent a kayak, make sure to enter the water from the pier area, rather than trying rough spots where you risk turning over on the lava. Kayakers are no longer allowed to go on the shore near the monument or pursue the spinner dolphins. Kayakers are now supplied with a set of rules intent on preserving this incredible area.

Whether you get here by a long swim, kayak, inflatable or with the popular Fair Wind excursion, you'll love the Captain Cook monument area with its three to ten-foot deep water near shore, dropping off into the deep indigo of the bay. To give you an idea of some of the sights: pufferfish, butterflyfish of all kinds (fourspot, raccoon, ornate, teardrop, milletseed, oval, reticulated), fantail filefish, Potter's angelfish, Triton's trumpet, eagle ray, turkeyfish, a variety of eels, triggerfish (Picasso, rectangular, lei), and much more.

The Captain Cook Monument, a 27-foot high white obelisk, marks the excellent snorkeling right in front. If you have a chance, explore the entire north side of Kealakekua Bay. The shallow cove to the west of the monument is an excellent snorkeling area and you may even see the elusive bronze plaque, marking the spot where Captain Cook supposedly died. High tide will cover the plaque completely, but it's near shore in this little cove.

GETTING THERE

Drive south on Highway 11 to almost the 111 mile marker (see area map, page 157). Watch for a Y with a small sign at Nāpō'opo'o Road. Head right, down the steep hill.

Some books suggest hiking to the monument from here—a locked gate blocks vehicles from the rugged, steep road. It's about a 1,500 foot drop to the water, the road is rough, indirect and unmarked, and there's no water available, so think long and hard before trying this. We talked to one couple who desperately tried to buy a ride up from the bottom with maintenance workers with no success.

It's a long, winding drive down the road to Nāpō'opo'o, but it's well worth it, as you wind through some strikingly beautiful greenery and flowers. At the bottom of the hill you drive directly ahead into the

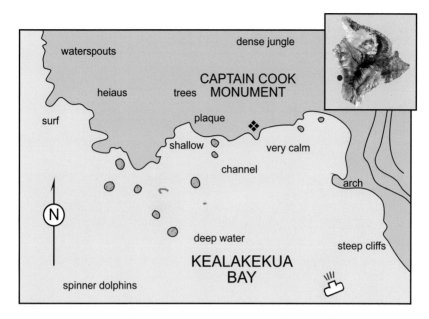

parking lot. To be a few hundred yards closer, it's also OK to turn right and park where the road ends, offering a nice view of the bay.

To the right of Kealakekua Park, you can see a rocky beach where entry to the water is quite easy. Reef shoes are needed because the beach has more pebbles and rocks than sand. It's possible to enter right at the end of the road, or walk to the far end and enter a bit closer to the monument. It just depends on whether you'd rather walk or swim. Enter from either the pier or this "beach" to swim across the bay to the monument area.

Just two boats currently have permission to anchor within the bay. Taking a comfortable boat that shades and feeds you is certainly a much easier way to get to the monument. In this particular case, we highly recommend the comfortable Fairwind II.

The water tends to be very calm here, even when rough elsewhere. Since the snorkeling is so superb, it's great to save your time and energy for this incredible spot, where two hours pass in a flash. If you're serious about snorkeling or even willing to try it once, don't even think about missing this opportunity. Try to spot some of the beautiful Potter's angelfish in the shallow areas near shore, or look sharp for an octopus.

Zodiac trips also stop at several spots around the bay; however, they tend to stay just a short time in each location. This spot really merits several hours. The Fair Wind II seems to spend just about the right amount of time.

Kealakekua Park

This is a small park at the north end of the road when you drive down the hill to Nāpōʻopoʻo. While the beach here is more pebbles than sand, it's often calm enough for good swimming and has good snorkeling to the left along the lava coast. Not as great as across the bay, but certainly worth checking out. If there are waves, stay beyond them for better visibility as well as safety. You'll find fairly large scattered coral heads in about fifteen feet of water from the "beach" to the pier on the left. Snorkeling is best to the left of the beach and extends out to about fifty yards from shore. A very strong swimmer can snorkel to the Captain Cook Monument from here.

GETTING THERE   Drive south on Highway 11 to just before 111 mile marker and watch for a Y with a small sign at Nāpōʻopoʻo Rd. (see area map, page 157). Head right, down the hill. Drive all the way down the hill through the lush jungle scenery. At the bottom, take a right turn and park at the end of the street—about a half block away. You'll see the park toward your right and the beach straight ahead. In winter the waves may be too rough, but conditions change often. When calm enough, snorkel from the beach to the left staying along the coast. The best snorkeling is between the pier and the "beach." For a VERY long snorkel, head to the right all the way to the Captain Cook Monument. Only very strong swimmers with good fins should attempt this swim.

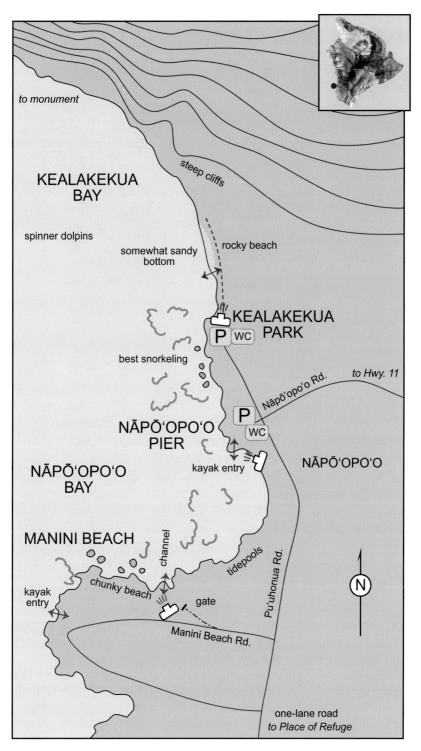

to monument

KEALAKEKUA
BAY

steep cliffs

spinner dolpins

somewhat sandy
bottom

rocky beach

KEALAKEKUA
PARK

P WC

best snorkeling

to Hwy. 11

Nāpō'opo'o Rd.

P
WC

NĀPŌ'OPO'O
PIER

NĀPŌ'OPO'O

kayak entry

NĀPŌ'OPO'O
BAY

MANINI BEACH

channel

tidepools

Pu'uhonua Rd.

kayak
entry

chunky beach

gate

N

Manini Beach Rd.

one-lane road
to Place of Refuge

Nāpōʻopoʻo Pier

The pier offers some parking and the easiest entry when the ocean is a bit rough at the beach. The pier may look too high for easy entry when tide is low, but there's a secret. Look at the picture above where a snorkeler sits on the steps that can't always be seen well from above. Snorkeling is best to the right within about fifty yards of the lava shoreline. You can also head to the left to explore a large area with scattered coral heads. Sometimes the fish will be plentiful all over this area, while other days are disappointing. Allow plenty of clearance when waves are crashing on the lava. When not too crowded, this pier is a good spot to launch a kayak for a memorable trip to the Captain Cook Monument. Weekends can bring gridlock to this small parking lot.

GETTING THERE   Drive south on Highway 11 to almost the 111 mile marker, watching for a Y with a small sign at Nāpōʻopoʻo Road (see area map, page 157). Head right, down the hill. Wind all the way down the hill through the lush jungle scenery and you will eventually hit the Nāpōʻopoʻo Pier parking lot—straight in front of you. Park in the gravel lot and walk out on the old pier (see site map, page 163). The steps and kayak launching area are located on the left side of the far end of the pier, where it is usually completely calm.

Picasso (lagoon) triggerfish

rectangular triggerfish

Manini Beach Park

This little public park has no facilities except picnic tables. The "beach" is really chunks of black lava and white coral. It's pretty, and there's an easy entry point if you're wearing booties. Otherwise, it's awfully sharp on the feet. The only snorkeling entry point is through a little channel (seen above) at the far right side of the beach. Angle to the right and snorkel out where there is enough clearance. Then continue to the right because the far left is usually rougher.

High tide is a real plus here for entry, because there's precious little clearance during low tide. Once out in the bay, there's plenty of space for comfort as you swim above the coral heads. Fish can be abundant or disappointing, depending on the day you snorkel, so that will affect your opinion of this bay.

The rest of this long beach (to the west) is too rocky for good swimming or snorkeling. Depending on the season and wave conditions, you may find some excellent tidepools just to the east.

Manini Park is a beautiful, peaceful spot for a picnic with views of the Captain Cook Monument area across the bay. Locals like to picnic here, so be respectful of their space. Watch for the many spinner dolphins who love to cavort in Kealakekua Bay.

GETTING THERE   Drive south on Highway 11 to almost the 111 mile marker (see area map, page 157), watching for a Y with a small sign at Nāpōʻopoʻo Rd. Head right, down the hill. Wind all the way down the hill through the lush jungle scenery (see map, page 163). At the bottom of the hill, take a left turn. Then, a quick right on narrow Manini Beach Rd. You'll pass a few houses before seeing the eastern corner of the park. Usually the entrance is chained. If so, just park along the street and walk the short way in. The snorkeling entry is near this entrance. Kayak entry is outside the park only.

Keʻei Beach

This well-hidden beach has excellent snorkeling when conditions are calm, but is often unsafe—especially in the winter. The coast is very rocky here and doesn't have the protection found in the nearby bays, so it isn't worth the rough drive unless you're certain swell is low. When calm, there's plenty of room to explore, with good coral, canyons, and arches. Just make sure you don't end up between a wave and some lava or coral. Keʻei is for experienced snorkelers only due to its isolation and exposure to waves. With a rental car, you may prefer to skip this very bumpy road.

GETTING THERE   Located between Kealakekua Bay and Hōnaunau Bay, access is from Puʻuhonua Rd. connecting these two bays (see area map, page 157). From the town of Nāpōʻopoʻo, take Puʻuhonua Rd. toward Place of Refuge (see map, page 163). Go about .5 of a mile from town, pass Keawaiki Rd. with its bunch of mailboxes, then take the next right toward the water.

Follow this bumpy road across the bare lava field as it turns left in about .2 of a mile, then continue another .2 of a mile. The road gets worse and worse, so you might as well park about here. If the sea is calm enough, you can enter from the lava here. Or, you can brave more poor road for another .2 of a mile to some picnic tables and another lava entry. Going the last bit to the sandy beach is hard on the car. Drive very slow and avoid this road after heavy rain. Local people will appreciate you driving slow since their houses are quite near the street, and children may be playing in the area.

The coast at Keʻei is quite rocky and mostly shallow, so we don't advise snorkeling unless conditions are extremely calm. Leave something in bright colors when you enter in order to find your way back for exit. You'll need to work your way around shallow areas to reach the more comfortable depth at the far edge of the reef.

Hōnaunau Bay (Two Step)

Located just a short walk north of Place of Refuge, this popular snorkeling site is one of the very best in the Hawaiʻian islands. The whole bay offers exciting and varied snorkeling. The shape of the bay provides good protection from swell, although the exit onto lava can be a bit challenging even with small swell. You need enough experience to exit onto the lava shore, so this isn't the place for timid first-time snorkelers unless the bay is really flat.

Two Step got it name from an entry point where there are two distinct bench-like ledges. We've marked the spot on our map (see page 169), but you're also likely to see local snorkelers and sun-bathers entering here unless you arrive very early (see picture, page 171). This smooth pahoehoe lava offers easy walking, but the sun heats it enough to require flip-flops in the summer.

Two Step has become very popular, so you'll need to come early to be assured of parking in the limited spots along the side of the road. When roadside parking fills, there's more nearby in the Place of Refuge lot, although you'll need to pay the very reasonable admission fee ($5 per car at the moment, but good for a week). Portapotties are available along the road, while restrooms and water are available near the exhibits in Place of Refuge.

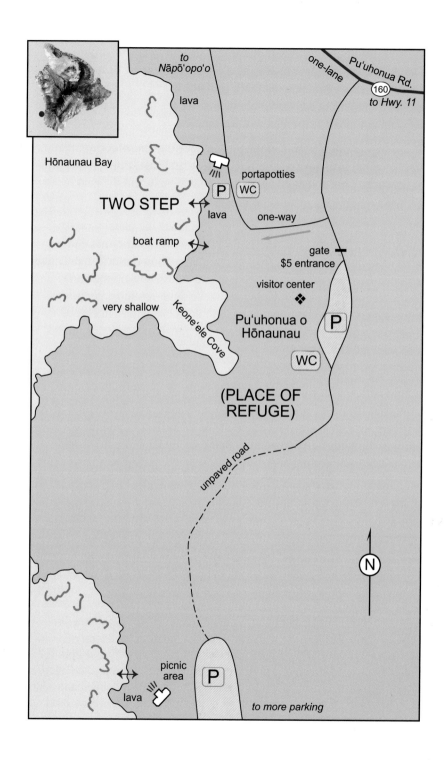

to
Nāpō'opo'o

lava

one-lane
Pu'uhonua Rd.
160
to Hwy. 11

Hōnaunau Bay

portapotties
P WC

TWO STEP ←→
lava
one-way

boat ramp ←→

gate
$5 entrance

visitor center

very shallow

Keone'ele Cove

Pu'uhonua o
Hōnaunau

P

WC

(PLACE OF
REFUGE)

unpaved road

N

picnic
area
P

lava

to more parking

169

All of Hōnaunau Bay is full of coral, fish, canyons, and arches. Depth ranges from five to fifty feet deep. If you want to stay in shallower water (about 5-10 feet), just snorkel to the right closer to the lava. Experienced snorkelers will enjoy the deeper canyons to the left and out close to the Place of Refuge.

If you're not comfortable exiting on lava or if swell picks up, the boat channel is always available. It's easy and safe, but very shallow at low tide. This is tucked between the lava entry and the park.

You're almost sure to see turtles here—especially where the water drops to twenty feet. And, of course, you'll see the usual wrasses, tangs, butterflyfish, eels, and even some larger pelagic fish. We've seen schools of more than fifty nocturnal raccoon butterflyfish lazing around. We even got lucky once and saw two white-tipped reef sharks cruising the outer deeper area. We once spotted a couple of titan triggerfish, something we haven't seen elsewhere in Hawai'i. Take our word for it; you'll want to return to Two Step every time you visit the Big Island.

There are no facilities other than the portapotties, a couple of shaded picnic tables, boat ramp, and a handful of parking spaces intended primarily for boat trailers. Just gorgeous views, a protected bay, great adjacent historical site, and some of the island's best and most varied snorkeling, with fairly easy entry and exit, make this a thoroughly outstanding snorkeling site.

Two Step is one of our personal favorite snorkeling sites in all of the Hawai'ian islands. It lacks a sandy beach and seclusion, but offers a great variety of sea life as well as fairly reliable conditions year round. It's also an excellent swimming spot with lovely surroundings. Don't miss this one! Help preserve it by using coverups such as lycra or wetsuits rather than sunscreen, which pollutes the water and poisons the fish and coral.

GETTING THERE

Drive south on Highway 11 from Kailua-Kona and turn right at the well-marked sign for Place of Refuge (Highway 160) at mile marker 104 (see area map, page 157). Follow this road down to the ocean and pass the entrance to Place of Refuge (see site map, page 169). About fifty feet past the entrance stay left along the ocean and you'll see Hōnaunau Bay with a boat ramp and some parking along the road. Park near the portapotties and picnic tables if space is available. Walk an easy hundred feet across the smooth black lava (pāhoehoe) and look for the best entry.

Unless you arrive very early, you'll find a cluster of snorkelers or divers at this spot. Don't make the mistake of trying to get in or out too far to the right. Look for the bench-like ledge to sit on while you pull on your fins. Then just step right in.

From Kealakekua Bay, you can take Pu'uhonua Road, a straight and narrow four-mile long road connecting the two bays. Pass the Y, turn right just before Place of Refuge, and you'll come to Two Step. Please be polite to the people who live here and have to put up with all these tourists every day. There are children at play, so slow down.

snorkeler entering at the 'Two Step' entry point

Place of Refuge

Puʻuhonua o Hōnaunau National Historical Park, called Place of Refuge by many books, offers excellent snorkeling from the lava picnic area, but only for experienced snorkelers. Swell can hit this unprotected shore and the lava entry isn't the easiest.

Still, there are plenty of large fish cruising by the area. We prefer to enter from the closest parking area in the long picnic area beyond the historical site. The picture above captures the challenge of entering here on a choppy day. Be sure to leave something on shore to mark your entry spot so that you can return to the same spot. Keep in mind that swell tends to get higher by noon, so come early if you can.

The black lava gets VERY hot during the day in the summer, so do wear something on your feet or you'll be hopping as you return to your car. One other caution is to watch for fishing lines—especially if you snorkel around the point to the right.

Place of Refuge itself is a serene and spiritual area, well worth the cost of parking. The information desk has an excellent brochure with map of the park and sells fish ID books as well as a large road map for the Big Island.

Due to the historical character of the park, beach users and snorkelers are not allowed to leave anything on the grounds (except for the picnic areas). It's still possible to enter the water through a canoe channel headed toward Two Step, however, we prefer to access that side entirely from Two Step.

GETTING THERE
From Highway 11 (see area map, page 157), drive south about seven miles past the Kealakekua turnoff. Take Highway 160 toward the water (between markers 103 and 104). It's an excellent road and well-marked. Near the water you'll see a sign on the left to the parking lot. Entrance is now five dollars.

Alternately, you can get from Nāpōʻopoʻo by taking the straight one-lane Puʻuhonua Road across the lava four miles south. It joins the highway near the entrance to the park.

Drive to the left of the information building at Place of Refuge (see site map, page 169). Instead of parking in the main lot, continue through to the far left of the parking onto a small road past two signs that say "picnic" and "no parking". It angles to the right toward the water, but looks like it goes nowhere.

Follow this road and you'll come upon a parking lot and picnic tables, with restrooms at the far end. Park here at the north (closest) end of the picnic area and walk straight toward the ocean across the smooth pāhoehoe lava. Watch the swell carefully before entering the water and definitely leave a easy to spot bag so that you can find the same location for your exit.

Picnic tables, shade and a lovely view are available here, but the restrooms and water are located at the end of the road to the south. Restrooms and water can also be found at the entrance to Place of Refuge. You will need shoes or flip-flops to cross the black lava in the middle of a hot summer day.

Hoʻokena Beach

Hoʻokena is one of several more distant beaches south of Kona and toward the southern tip of the island. Most of these can be snorkeled only in calm weather, so check out conditions carefully before snorkeling. Water conditions are dependent on the direction of the waves and can sometimes be fine even during stormy winter months when wind direction changes—sometimes quite suddenly.

Hoʻokena is a relatively sheltered long sand beach with snorkeling amid the rocks in all directions. It does have restrooms, showers, palms, some tidepools and boat entry, although the facilities are fairly basic and not always clean. Walking or driving to the right will take you to Keālia Beach which is poor for swimming, but good for experienced snorkelers because of its wide, shallow coral shelf.

GETTING THERE   Driving south on Highway 11 (see map, page 157), go 2.6 miles past the Highway 160 turnoff, which heads for Place of Refuge. The Hoʻokena turnoff is well-marked, so it's easy to find. Follow this paved road 2.3 miles toward the water at the end. It's only one and a half lanes wide and winding, but easy to drive. The best access to the beach is found at the end of the tiny one-lane Y to the left as you approach the water.

raccoon butterflyfish

South Area

The southern point of the Big Island is located in the Kaʻū district. This austere, windswept corner of the island is the most southern land in all fifty states—even further south than Puerto Rico. While it isn't the Big Island's prettiest corner (for much of it is quite barren due to the strong winds), it's dramatic and worth a look. Be sure to visit the high cliffs with long ladders where ships used to be loaded. This looks like an unlikely place for loading and unloading, but it was used long before dredged harbors were available. Back then the deep water just off shore made it possible for the larger boats to get close to shore. This must have been challenging—to say the least.

Bays along this southern coast offer some good snorkeling, but only when swell isn't rolling in from the South Pacific. Check the weather report before counting on water sports of any kind along the south coast—especially in the summer. Mahana Bay (Green Sand Beach) is

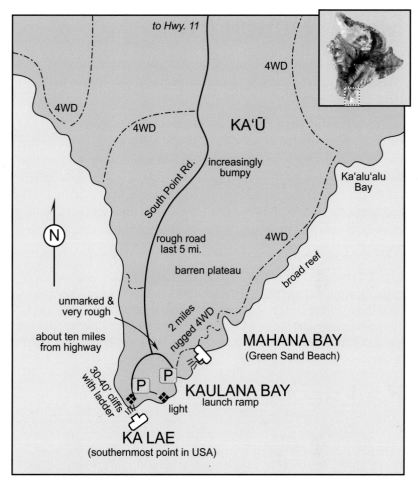

very exposed to the south, but still worth the long hike. Just stay out of the water here if there's any doubt.

Kaulana Bay is much more protected, but not nearly as pretty. Punaluʻu (Black Sand Beach) is a popular tourist stop, but is typically too rough for safe snorkeling or swimming. Ka Lae can be challenging unless very calm—at least when approached from the ladder. Save this one for the locals unless climbing crude ladders doesn't bother you, or come by boat if you ever have a chance. Even then, watch out for swift currents that can run along the shore.

Whittington Park is another somewhat protected site in the south, but best left to experienced snorkelers unless unusally calm. We continue in a counter-clockwise direction around the dramatic southern coast of Hawaiʻi.

Miloli'i Beach Park

For the public beach on Miloli'i Bay, just follow the signs to Miloli'i Beach Park. Snorkel here in calm weather only; there's lots to see right near the shore.

We've heard that Papa Bay just north has excellent snorkeling at the far right. We hesitated to try it because it's necessary to cross through the residential section to the right when you reach the bottom of the hill. Signs at each street to the right state "Private subdivision, not a public access, residents and authorized persons only, violators will be prosecuted". This neighborhood is Hawai'ian Lands and prefers its privacy. Snorkeling or diving from a boat would be a better way to access this site.

GETTING THERE   On Highway 11 (see road map, page 5), pass marker 89, then watch for the Miloli'i sign. The steep road down to the beach starts out as a newly-paved one-lane road, then becomes older and even narrower as it switches back and forth. It's about five miles down with some local traffic (uphill has the right-of-way), so go nice and slow.

Ka Lae (South Point)

While wind-swept Ka Lae (the southernmost land in the USA) barely qualifies as a snorkeling or swimming site, it does deserve a mention. Go to see the bare and beautiful south end of the island. We would recommend you think twice before climbing down the tall iron ladder to swim. However, it's possible by boat when the seas are calm enough out in the channel.

If there's any swell at all, this area could have stiff currents, so stay out of the water. Come to look only. That said, we've been to the ladders on a very stormy day only to find the water at the base of the cliff calm and clear as a swimming pool. Waves were smashing against each other nearby in the channel, but this popular fishing area near the ladder was quite calm—as you can see in the picture. But please, VERY experienced snorkelers only. If you choose to try the ladders, do so with great care, and not alone.

178

GETTING THERE   Heading south on Highway 11 (see area map, page 177), take South Point Road past the wind farms on bumpy and narrow asphalt, then angle right to the end of the road where you'll find parking above the ladder that drops down 30-40 feet to the water. No facilities or shade here, but a VERY dramatic cliff dropping straight into clear water. And a usually choppy channel not far from shore.

Kaulana Bay

Kaulana Bay is a nice sheltered place for a quick dip or snorkel when visiting Ka Lae (South Point). Best when south winds and surf are low, but relatively sheltered from the waves inside the cove. Although not the island's most picturesque spot, we enjoy the snorkeling in this small bay and have seen plenty—including a snowflake eel, Hawai'ian hogfish and huge schools of whiteband surgeonfish. Unfortunately, summer swell often hits from the south, so Kaulana can be choppy just when you're in the mood to cool off. Stay within the points if in doubt about offshore currents. When calm, you'll see children playing near the ramp and their parents fishing from the sides.

You'll find ample parking in the gravel lot at the edge of the beach and more further up the hill (if you don't want to drive on the roughest area). There are no facilities near Kaulana and no shelter from the sun, except for one small tree near the ramp.

GETTING THERE

Take Highway 11 from Kailua-Kona toward the far south of the island. Turn right on South Point Road (see area map, page 177). Pass the wind farms as the narrow asphalt road gets bumpier, then take a left at the unmarked Y near the ocean rather than right toward the point. This one-lane gravel road to the left will wind toward Kaulana Bay (about ten miles south of Highway 11), as the gravel road gets increasingly rutted. We drive to the bay, but you may want to park overlooking the bay and walk the last little bit of rough road.

Entry is easiest from the old concrete boat ramp on the left, providing you don't slip on the algae. Snorkel anywhere within the small bay, venturing beyond the points ONLY if you have exceptionally calm weather. Watch carefully for offshore currents in the deeper water beyond the points. Pelagic fish cruise the points, so you may see some larger creatures that the fishers hope to catch. Our picture shows how calm this little bay can be on a day when the channel was full of white caps.

ornate wrasse

Mahana Bay (Green Sand Beach)

This dramatic and unusual drive shouldn't be attempted by anything you can rent from the regular car companies—not even regular 4WD, due to the very deep ruts. Some big local 4WD vehicles can make the trip over the deeply-rutted barren landscape, but just barely. There are some locals who make a business of shuttling people out there for a small fee. It does make an interesting and beautiful trip.

If you're feeling energetic, hike the two miles over barren, windswept terrain passing interesting historical sites along the way—a great excuse to rest. Basically, all trails to the east lead to the same place. You can't miss Green Sands Beach. It's a dramatic crater, dropping down from the plateau, with greenish olivine sand and an enticing beach with good snorkeling and swimming when calm.

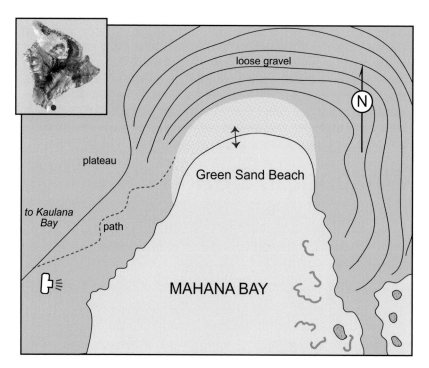

This is not the place for beginners unless seas are completely calm, but it's a delightful location when the weather is decent. Take rugged shoes, sun protection and plenty of water. After such a long hike, why not stay for a picnic too?

Green Sands is unique and has good snorkeling—especially to the left. Entry is easy from the sand as long as swell isn't too high. Swimmers and beginners should remain close to shore, but experienced snorkelers can wander around the rocks IF conditions are safe (not like in our picture). Keep in mind that big south swell tends to arrive in the summer from storms in the South Pacific. And these big waves bring dangerous offshore currents. Check on surf conditions before the hike, because it's a shame to trek two hot miles and not be able to at least swim in this dramatic and gorgeous bay.

GETTING THERE

Head south from Kailua-Kona and take Highway 11 to the turnoff for Ka Lae (South Point) to the right. As you near the ocean, take the narrow Y to the left that leads to Kaulana Bay with a small boat ramp at the end of the road (see area map, page 177). The dirt road gets increasingly rutted, so you may want to park above the cove. Park here on the dirt and hike down on the bumpy road to the cove. For the two-mile trek to Green Sands, continue to the left (east) starting next to the boat ramp.

183

The trail has numerous branches as it passes the old stone walls, but stay fairly close to the water and you'll easily spot the dramatic green sand crater. Last time we were there, a pole marked the path down. The trail down to the beach is about 300 yards and not as difficult as it appears from the top. The beach is beautiful, but offers no shade in the middle of the day. Enter from the sand at the center of the beach and snorkel to the left and around the rocks as far as seems safe. Take care climbing the crater because rescue isn't easy out here.

Whittington Beach Park

Whittington Beach Park has a row of several lovely beaches with covered picnic sites, facilities and shallow tidepools. Most of this coast is lava, so access is tricky, especially if there are any waves at all. Plenty of wind hits this southern part of the island.

The best spot to enter the water is just left of the old wharf (at the far right of the park), where the sea tends to be more protected. Swim around the wharf to the right and snorkel the rocks to the right of this small bay. The entry here over lava and coral is definitely not for

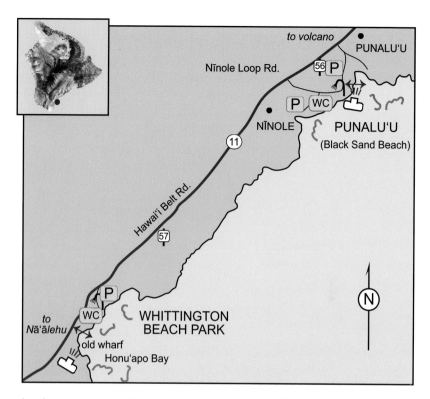

beginners—especially when there are waves. Watch very carefully for the wind direction and currents. Ask local people for advice whenever possible; there are usually local families picnicking, and sometimes scuba diving groups.

Keep in mind that locals may find the ocean much easier than you do when there is a big swell because they've had more practice. It's not always as easy as you think to keep from getting scraped (or worse) on the coral when a wave suddenly arrives (see Understanding Waves, page 27). Check swell size from the south before heading to this area. Restrooms, showers, shade, and picnic tables are available toward the west side of the park, but no drinking water.

GETTING THERE   From Kailua-Kona, head south on Highway 11 past South Point (see road map, page 6). Eventually the highway comes close to the water at Whittington, which is along the right. As you come down a hill and see water near the highway, watch carefully. There is a sign, but it's set about twenty-five feet off the highway, so it's easy to sail on by. You have to make a sharp right at the sign and double back about 1/4 of a mile to the large parking area. All facilities are found just to the west of the parking.

Punaluʻu (Black Sand Beach)

A popular (somewhat overrated) spot to stop on the way to the volcano, Punaluʻu Beach Park offers showers, restrooms, camping, phone, even drinking water. The black-sand beach has a boat ramp at the northeastern end where you can enter the water, but only on a very calm day. When wind and south swell pick up, stay close to shore because currents can be strong along the unprotected south coast. A rocky beach adds to the challenge. Often you must settle for the view and the sight of turtles grazing on the rocks.

GETTING THERE   As Highway 11 passes South Point and swings back toward Hilo, the highway passes close to Black Sand Beach. It's just to the north of Nīnole (see map, page 185). Not a bad place to take a break on a trip to the volcano (if coming from the south). It's close to Highway 11, and well-marked.

Snorkeling Grad School

We know some of you will progress to advanced snorkeling. Here are a few tips gleaned from our thousands of happy hours paddling around in the salty seas.

Now that you know many of the common fish of Hawai'i, take it up a notch or two by going places you might have neglected, such as shallow rocky areas, the surge zone, and deep dropoffs. You'll begin to see fish and critters that are not depicted on those plastic fish guides. If you have a curious nature, it's tons of fun.

We love to snorkel in the shallow areas at the fringes of many bays. At some sites, this may be 2 to 5-foot deep rubble, not very pretty at first glance. But if you are patient, and look closely, here is where you'll find the spectacular snowflake moray eel, octopus, Picasso triggerfish, cute tiny juvenile stages of reef fish such as the yellowtail coris (which looks a lot like Nemo) and sailfin tangs. You may see shelled molluscs of many types (stay clear of cone shells!), and perhaps some shell-less snails, such as the fried egg and clumped nudibranches, or the brightly colored one inch long fuschia flatworm. This is a good way to enjoy the water when swell has stirred up sediment, as it looks good even in 20-foot visibility conditions because you're so close.

The surge zone is rarely visited by divers, so you'll spot fish there they seldom see. Beautiful sailfin tangs, spotted surgeonfish, Christmas wrasses, bluefin trevallies and occasional big surge wrasses love the constant wave action of the surge zone. You must use extra caution here, as wave action can throw you against the coral or rocks. Remember that periodic sets of bigger swell are likely, so always have an exit strategy, and be careful to not be in a spot where big waves could trap you.

As you venture further out at the edges of many sites, you'll enter the area of deep dropoffs. Swimming along the steep rocky walls, you're likely to see pelagic fish, such as ulua, leatherbacks, spotted eagle rays, and even an occasional manta ray. Watch out for currents, as they are more common and can be faster as you near the points of a bay. Don't take a trip to Tahiti!

You are unlikely to see all the fish that live in Hawai'i in just one lifetime: but it's worth a try. Are you having fun yet?

East Area

Continuing around the island in counterclockwise direction, we come to the east, which includes Puna and South Hilo. These beaches are rather remote from where most tourists stay, but some sites are well worth a try if you are passing here on a good day (that is, low swell from the east or south).

Puna, in the southeastern corner of the Big Island, is about as far as you can get from the major tourist areas. You may want to combine a visit to the volcanoes with a snorkeling break in a series of swimming-pool sized tidepools. The Puna area is scenic, has several large parks, and plenty to do. Visit the volcano area on your way; check out Lava Tree Monument; lunch in the small town of Pāhoa; soak in the hot springs at Isaac Hale Beach Park; or snorkel in the unusual tidepools at Waiʻōpae.

Consider staying through the evening in order to drive down Chain of Craters Road at sunset to see the flowing red-orange lava after dark. Check first with park rangers for the latest information as to whether any lava is flowing, and where you can park closest to it. If you're lucky, you may be able to hike across the hardened lava to see the newest lava up close. A truly unforgettable experience. At times the lava flow can barely be seen through binoculars. There is no road connecting the coast across this active flow. We've been to Chain of

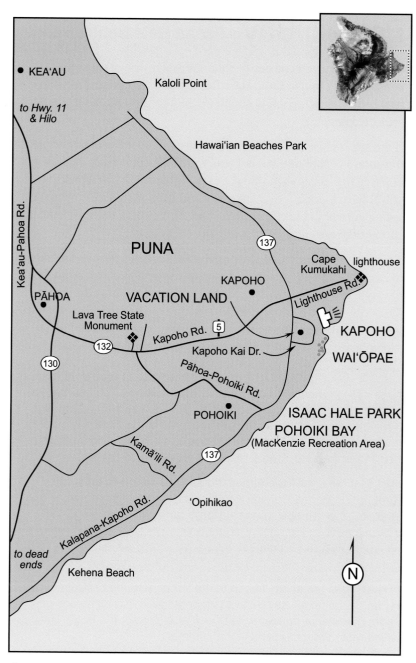

Craters Road when we could walk right up to the red flowing lava (close enough to melt our soles); other times we could barely see lava a mile away; and once the crater road was closed to all traffic. Call ahead if your goal is to see some flowing lava (808 961-8093).

Pohoiki Bay (Isaac Hale Beach Park)

On a calm day you can easily enter the water to snorkel at the popular boat ramp at Isaac Hale Beach Park. Watch carefully for boat traffic, which is fairly frequent. Snorkel straight out into a very protected area.

If the sea is close to flat, you can snorkel to the left around the pier to venture further out. It's not really difficult snorkeling, but always requires fins even when it looks easy. When south swell picks up, you'll have to look it over carefully and keep in mind there can be a strong current in the center of the bay. Large south swell also creates strong offshore currents all along the south coast.

This park is an attractive and popular place with lush surroundings to explore—including natural volcano-warmed fresh water pools in the lava. Facing the sea, a small path leads off towards the right to the pools, where warm water bubbles into the lava pools surrounded by jungle greenery. No showers or drinking water here, but plenty of sandy beach.

GETTING THERE   Take Highway 11 (see area map, page 189) to Highway 130 (Kea'au-Pāhoa Road). The intersection is at the town of Kea'au. Head south on Highway 130, a beautiful tree-lined drive with smooth pavement. At Pāhoa, continue straight toward the water on Highway 132 through a lush overgrown area. Don't take the Lava Tree turnoff that you'll see on the left.

Just past the Lava Tree turnoff, hold to the right (left leads to Kapoho) on Pāhoa-Pohoiki Road, which eventually narrows to one lane. You'll arrive at a wonderful large park (see map, page 193). You can park on the right near the boat entry area at the breakwater where ithe sea is calmest. It's a very short walk out on the little breakwater if you want to check out conditions from the end.

Snorkel from the sandy beach to the left around the breakwater as far as it is calm. Always be alert for boat traffic as well as any offshore currents or riptides when swell arrives from the South Pacific, which most often happens in the summer.

Snuba

Snuba was developed as a simpler alternative to scuba for shallow dives in resort conditions. Because Snuba divers are strictly limited in depth and conditions, and are always accompanied by a guide, the orientation takes just 15-30 minutes.

Two people share a small inflatable raft, which holds a scuba air tank. A twenty-foot hose leads from the tank to a light harness on each diver. A comfortable weight belt completes your outfit. Very light and tropical!

Once in the water, your guide teaches you to breathe through your regulator (which has a mouthpiece just like your snorkel) on the surface until you're completely comfortable. You're then free to swim around as you like, remembering to clear your ears as needed (limited by the hose to twenty feet deep, of course).

The raft will automatically follow you as you tour the reef. It's that easy! You have to be at least eight years old, and have normal good health. Kids do amazingly well, and senior citizens can also enjoy Snuba. There's even a new program called Snuba Doo for four to seven-year-old children. They wear a flotation vest, and breathe through a regulator as they float on the surface while their parents Snuba below.

We are certified scuba divers, yet we often enjoy Snuba more. Less gear equals more fun. Snuba is a lot like snorkeling, with the added freedom to get down close to fish and coral. We often surface dive to check out what fish is hiding under a coral head. Snuba is like surface diving without having to come up for air!

Snuba provides a fun and safe experience if you pay attention and do it as directed. Their safety record is superb.

Warning: do pay attention to the instructions because even at these shallow depths, you must know the proper way to surface. You must remember to never hold your breath as you ascend or you could force a bubble of air into your blood. Breathing out continually while surfacing is not intuitive, but is absolutely necessary when you're breathing compressed air. This is especially important to remember if you're used to surface diving where you always hold your breath. Dive safely!

Wai'ōpae Tidepools (Kapoho Bay)

The Wai'ōpae tidepools area is at the Vacation Land development just west of Kapoho Bay—Kapoho means depression in Hawai'ian. This is a magical and unique place where you can snorkel in large interconnecting lava tidepools with unusual and very colorful coral and lots of smallish fish. The area is entirely protected by a long natural lava breakwater. In the tidepools, you'll see coral unique to this area, which makes it well worth a long side trip if you're anywhere in the vicinity. Open 7 a.m. to 7 p.m. only.

A local resident told us that visitors are welcome as long as they do not litter or damage these precious tidepools, which are still in excellent condition. We urge you to heed this local sentiment, and treat the tidepools with great care.

The tidepools are completely protected from pounding waves, getting no swell or currents other than the tide coming and going. Any junk that goes in, tends to stay in. "Take only pictures, and leave only footprints" would be a good idea here. If you find any litter, please take it out with you.

There are no facilities at all, so come prepared. Walk out over the lava wearing shoes—this is somewhat rough lava and you will want to walk about 2/3 of the way toward the breaking waves (about two

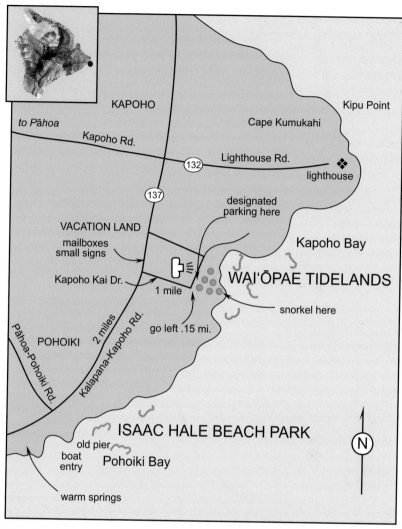

hundred yards). The first tidepools you see are quite shallow, but as you proceed, they become deeper and more interesting. The best time to snorkel the tidepools is at high tide, because it's easier to glide from pool to pool. Check which way the tide is going and follow it, rather than swimming against it.

Reef shoes or booties are better than fins here because they enable you to snorkel one pool, and then climb over to another—which is especially useful if the tide is low. Old athletic shoes or any kind of plastic shoes will suffice if you don't have any reef shoes. Many folks wear fins, which definitely aren't needed or wanted since the pools are small (with only a few bigger than swimming pools).

It's a little slippery getting in and you need to watch for a few sea urchins, but once in, the snorkeling is easy and captivating. The coral is green, pink, and purple—the most colorful and unusual we've seen in Hawai'i. The water is clear, calm and only about five-feet deep so you can examine the coral up close. This is ideal for beginners who have enough control to avoid touching the coral.

GETTING THERE

From Isaac Hale (see map, page 189), take Highway 137 north about two miles until you see mailboxes on the left and a gravel road on the right (Kapoho Kai Road). Take a right here at a little sign that says "Vacation Land" and "private road". Continue one mile to the end of this road. When the road curves 90° at the water, take a left on an even smaller road (Wai'ōpae Road) for .15 of a mile until you can see the tidepools. There is now a small designated public parking area for about 15 cars. This often fills early on weekends and holidays. There is no other legal parking nearby.

From Kapoho (see site map, page 193), take 130 and follow the signs to Kapoho. Stay left on Highway 132 just past the Lava Tree exit. Kapoho also has excellent tidepools, but is private and has actually posted a guard, so you need to head south along the beach road (137) 1.15 miles until you see the cluster of mailboxes on the right, then take Kapoho Kai Rd. (a gravel road with a little sign that says "Vacation Land" and another "private road") to the left for 1 mile to the end, then a left on an even smaller road (Wai'ōpae Road) for .15 of a mile until you see the tidepools with parking directly in front.

Hilo

Dramatic Hilo, built mostly on black lava, used to be the most popular tourist destination on the Big Island. Set in the beautiful, jungle green, rainy side of Hawai'i, it is an area that seems in a time warp. Most tourists now prefer the sun-filled days on the leeward side of the island. Hilo is just the opposite in climate, getting rain 278 days a year. Hilo is worth at least a day-trip, if only to see how lovely Hawai'i used to be.

You'll probably want to visit Hilo for other reasons, but there is surprisingly good snorkeling available, weather permitting—especially at protected Richardson Beach Park (page 196). You do have to be prepared to snorkel in the rain, not a problem except that it can be a bit cooler over here. Since Hilo's beaches face the prevailing northeast trade winds, they need protection to be calm enough for either swimming or snorkeling. In Hilo the exposed beaches are better for surfing. And the many shallow ones are best for wading.

If you drive to Hilo, be sure to spend some time in town. Shop a bit, stop for lunch, and enjoy the quieter atmosphere as well as the great beauty on this side of the island. Akaka Falls and the Hawai'i Tropical Botanical Garden (both north of Hilo) are just two of the attractions you won't want to miss.

Drive to Hilo either by way of Waimea or the Saddle Road (similar distance either way). While many car rental firms don't want you on the Saddle Road, it's a perfectly passable, and has some interesting vegetation as you drive through many climate zones. The Hilo half has been fully updated, but work continues on the Kona half, which is still a paved one-lane road with a double line down the center. But it has VERY little traffic.

The Saddle Road has no available gas or help should you have car trouble. Don't expect any sympathy or assistance from your car rental company if you break down up here. The Saddle Road also takes you to the road heading up to Mauna Kea to see the unbelievable number of stars that are visible most nights. That's assuming a rare snowstorm doesn't close the steep access road. Allow plenty of time with a stop at the shop part way up (to adjust to the altitude) and be sure to bring your warmest clothing!

arc-eye hawkfish

Richardson Beach Park

Many guides say that there is no snorkeling near Hilo. Not true. There is a row of similar shallow beaches very close to town—all of them along Kalaniana'ole Street (Highway 137) and very close together. Of the bunch, Richardson Park is definitely our choice.

Snorkel near shore where entry is easy from the tiny beach seen in the picture above. You can snorkel either direction. The large, near-shore area is well-protected by the natural breakwater. Surfers enjoy the unprotected open area.

The water can be a bit cooler here due to fresh water springs common at many Big Island snorkeling sites. Patches of fresh water are also the cause of the patches of oily-looking water (see Doctor my Eyes, page 73). Just keep swimming and the temperature and clarity will change. Visibility tends to be worse on this side, due to the heavier swell action and rainwater runoff. If you hit a patch of weather that turns this side relatively calm, and you are near Hilo, give it a try.

When choppy, this is not a beach for a person who likes to keep some space between their body and the coral. Most of it is fairly shallow, especially at low tide. There's actually enough clearance, but not for the claustrophobic. One cool rainy day, when we were snorkeling

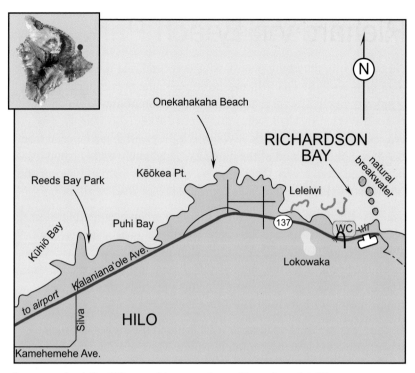

Onekahakaha Beach

RICHARDSON BAY

natural breakwater

N

Reeds Bay Park

Kēōkea Pt.

Leleiwi

Puhi Bay

137

WC

Kūhiō Bay

Kalanianaʻole Ave.

Lokowaka

to airport

Silva

HILO

Kamehemehe Ave.

here, we had the lifeguard to ourselves. He enjoyed telling us more about the many fish we had seen and seemed genuinely happy to have some visitors.

If you just want a cooling dip, the other nearby beaches are mostly fine. The tidepools look inviting, but some are no longer clean, and have posted signs warning you to keep out. A refreshing swim and shower are welcome, especially if you've driven all the way from Kailua-Kona to see the Hilo area. Don't let a little rain keep you from trying this pretty spot. When the sun's out, the deep shade and small lawn are welcome.

GETTING THERE   Cross the island to Hilo (see maps, pages 6 and 196). From the corner of Highway 11 and Kalanianaʻole Street. (the northwest corner of the Hilo Airport), take Kalanianaʻole Street. east along the shore. Drive 3.7 miles, passing Reed Bay, Puhi, Onekahakaha, Leleiwi, with lots of tidepools and shallow reef.

Park in the little Richardson parking lot and walk toward the water. Showers and restrooms are available on the left close to the parking lot. Just behind the house on your right, walk until you see the hidden lifeguard station. It's not far at all, just hidden by the lush Hilo vegetation. Come early on weekends or holidays.

197

Waipiʻo Valley

North of Hilo, the going gets slow as you head into the Hamakua district, with its steep cliffs and exposure to the prevailing northeast wind and swell. The more northeastern section of the Big Island is not traversed by road—the valleys cut through too sharply. The biggest valley of this series is Waipiʻo Valley and it can be seen from the overlook at the end of the highway. This lovely valley can only be reached from a very steep road by way of the town of Kukuihaele, where excursions are available for tourists (see road map, page 6).

Waipiʻo Beach can have decent snorkeling when weather permits, but that's very rare, since the rugged northeast coast catches heavy swell much of the year. Besides, coral growth is limited in areas that catch the brunt of northeastern swells. Leave this one to the locals. You're better off spending your time on a hiking tour of the lush jungle valley with its twin 1200-foot waterfalls.

If you've come to Hāmākua, at least drive to the end of the road, where you can view this dramatic valley. Most of Hāmākua is bordered by high cliff allowing little safe water access, but delightful views from the highway when the sky is clear. Check out Akaka Falls and the spectacular botanical garden both accessible from the coast highway north of Hilo.

goldrim surgeonfish

199

Marine Life

The coral reef supports tremendous diversity in a small space. On a healthy reef, you've never seen everything, because of the boggling variety of species, as well as changes from day to day and changes from day to night. The reef functions much like the oasis in the desert providing food (more abundant than the open ocean) and shelter from predators. Only the wild rain forests can compare with the reef in complexity.

In Hawai'i the coral reef itself is less spectacular than in warmer waters of the world. This is counterbalanced by the colorful and abundant fish, which provide quite a show.

There are excellent color fish identification cards available in bookstores and dive shops. We particularly like the ones published by Natural World Press. There are also many good marine life books that give far more detailed descriptions of each creature than we attempt in these brief notes.

OCTOPUS

Some varieties of octopuses hide during the day while others hunt by day. They eat shrimp, fish, crabs, and mollusks—you should eat so well! Octopuses have strong beaks and can bite humans, so it's safer to not handle them.

Hawai'ian day octopus

Being mollusks without shells, they must rely on speed, cunning and camouflage to escape danger. Octopuses are capable of imitating a flashing sign, or changing their color and texture to match their surroundings in an instant. This makes them very hard to spot, even when they're hiding in plain sight—usually on the

Hawai'ian night octopus

bottom or on rocks. They can squirt ink to confuse predators. They only live about two years.

Just because you haven't seen one does not mean they aren't there. Go slow and watch carefully for a rock or coral that moves. It may take you some time to find one (weeks? months?) but when you do, it is a real thrill.

SHRIMP

In all kinds, colors, and sizes, they like to hide in rocks and coral—often living symbiotically with the coral. They are difficult to spot during the daytime, but at night you will notice lots of tiny pairs of eyes reflected in the flashlight beam. Most are fairly small and well-disguised.

banded coral shrimp

Some examples include: the harlequin shrimp (brightly colored) that eat sea stars, the banded coral shrimp (found all over the world), and numerous tiny shrimp that you won't see without magnification.

SEA URCHINS

Concealed tube feet allow urchins to move around in their hunt for algae. The collector urchin has pebbles and bits of coral attached for camouflage. These urchins are quite common in Hawai'i, and have no hazardous spines.

Beware of purple-black urchins with long spines. These are common in shallow water at many beaches. It's not the long spines that get you, it's the razor-sharp ones hidden beneath. The bright red pencil sea urchin is common and easy to spot. Although large, its spines aren't nearly sharp enough to be a problem for people. The spines can actually be used for chalk.

banded sea urchin

SEA STARS

brittle star

Abundant, but not seen much by snorkelers. The crown-of-thorns sea star, which has venomous spines, is found in Hawai'i, but not in large numbers like the South Pacific. Sea stars firmly grasp their prey with strong suction cups, and then eat at their leisure.

RAYS

manta ray

Manta rays (large plankton-eaters) use two flaps to guide plankton into their huge efficient mouths. Mantas often grow to be two meters from wing-tip to wing-tip, and can weigh 300 pounds. They can't sting, and are a real treat to watch.

Mantas feed at night by doing forward rolls in the water with mouths wide open. Lights will attract plankton which appeal to the manta rays. Dive boats can attract manta rays with their bright lights making the night trips to see these creatures very exciting.

Another beautiful ray, the spotted eagle ray, can sometimes be seen cruising the bottom for food and can grow to be seven feet across. They have a dark back with lots of small white dots and an extremely long tail. Their fins function more like wings so they seem to be flying along rather than swimming.

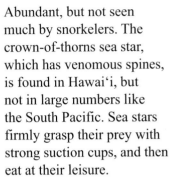

spotted eagle ray

Common sting rays prefer the sandy bottom and usually stay in calm, shallow, warmer water, where they can evade people.

EELS

Many types of moray eels abound among the reefs of Hawai'i. Some can grow to two meters long. While you may not see any on a given day, you can be sure they are all around the reef hiding in crevices.

whitemouth moray eel

Varieties of moray found in Hawai'i include undulated, whitemouth, snowflake, zebra (black and white stripes), wavy-lined, mottled, and dragon moray (often reddish-brown with distinct white spots of differing sizes).

Morays prefer to hide in holes during the day. If out cruising, they often find a nearby hole when spotting a snorkeler. When they stick out their heads and breathe, their teeth are most impressive.

undulated moray eel

Eels generally have no interest in eating snorkelers, other than very pushy and annoying ones, while they are quite able to swallow a fairly large fish. Please avoid putting your hands into reef crevices, since this is a great way to spend the afternoon getting stitches.

203

TRUMPETFISH

These long, skinny fish can change color, often bright yellow, light green with shaded bars, or light blue—and will change color in front of your eyes. They sometimes hang upright to blend with their

trumpetfish

environment, lying in wait to suck in their prey. They also shadow other fish and change their color to sneak up on prey—even at a cleaning station. They can be yellow, black, green with lines, or nearly transparent.

They do eat throughout the day, which is unusual for fish-eaters, who usually eat at dawn or dusk. Trumpetfish are quite common in Hawai'i and often seen hanging out alone. Some grow to more than one meter long, and can vacuum up surprisingly big fish.

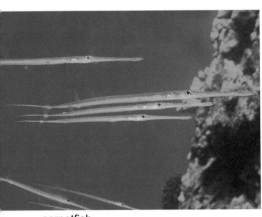

cornetfish

Cornetfish are similar to trumpetfish in shape and size, but have a distinctive thin filament extending from the center of the tail. Sometimes small cornetfish can be seen in big groups. Adults can be grow to be even larger than trumpetfish and can also change color quickly.

NEEDLEFISH

These pointed, common silvery-blue fish always swim very near the surface, usually in schools—occasionally leaping from the water. All types of needlefish are long and skinny as their name implies, and grow to as much as two feet long. Color and markings vary, but the long narrow shape is distinctive and hard to mistake. They're usually bluish on top, and translucent below for camouflage. They are common in shallow, calm water.

BUTTERFLYFISH

Butterflyfish are beautiful, colorful, abundant and varied in Hawaiʻi. They have incredible coloration, typically bright yellow, white, orange, black, and sometimes a little blue or red. They hang out near coral, eating algae, sponges, tube worms and very small coral polyps.

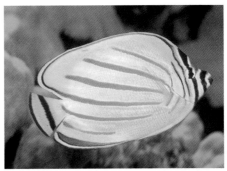
ornate butterflyfish

No one really understands the purpose of their beautiful colors, but many have speculated. Perhaps they serve territorial or mating needs.

threadfin butterflyfish

Juveniles are often distinctly different in coloring. Bizarre patterns may confuse predators—especially since they can pivot fast. Bars may help some hide, while stripes are seen more in faster fish. Black lines across the eyes and spots near the tail may also confuse predators.

multiband butterflyfish

Butterflyfish are often seen in pairs remaining together for up to three years. They're all delightful to watch. Hovering and turning are more important to them than speed since they stay near shelter of the reef and catch a quick meal—like a tube worm.

longnose butterflyfish

saddleback butterflyfish

reticulated butterflyfish

fourspot butterflyfish

teardrop butterflyfish

The ones you are most likely to see while snorkeling in Hawai'i include: raccoon (reminding you of the face of the animal), ornate (with bright orange lines making it easy to spot), threadfin (with diagonal lines), saddleback (fairly rare), lemon (very tiny), bluestripe (a beautiful one found only in Hawai'i), fourspot, milletseed, teardrop, and forceps (also called longnose).

The lined butterflyfish is the largest variety found in Hawai'i. The reticulated, often found in the surge zone, are not common, but are particularly beautiful. The smaller ovals (found in pairs scattered around on most reefs) seem to glow from within, especially on a sunny day.

Many butterflyfish have black spots across the eyes and near the tail—perhaps to confuse a predator about which way they're headed. Watch and they may confuse you too.

Most butterflyfish are common near the reef and pay little attention to snorkelers so they're fun to watch and often easy to identify with their distinctive markings.

PARROTFISH

Among the most dramatically colored fish on the reef, male parrotfish are blue, green, turquoise, yellow, lavender, and/or orange with endless variations of these colors. Females tend to be a more drab reddish brown. No two are alike. Parrotfish are very beautiful, with artistic, abstract markings.

female parrotfish

These fish change colors at different times in their lives and can also change sex as needed. They can be quite large (up to one meter).

male parrotfish

Patient grazers, they spend countless hours scraping algae from dead coral with their large, beak-like teeth, and create tons of white sand in the process. Most prefer to zoom away from snorkelers, but you'll see them passing gracefully by and will hear them crunching away at the coral. Unfortunately they are heavily fished, so less numerous lately.

Picasso (lagoon) triggerfish

TRIGGERFISH

Fond of sea urchins as a main course, triggerfish graze during the day on algae, worms and other small items.

Varieties include the Picasso (wildly colorful—quite rare at many sites, but worth watching for), reef (the Hawai'ian state fish), pinktail (easy to identify with its black body, white fins and pink tail), black (common, distinctive white lines between body and fins). The checkerboard triggerfish has a pink tail, yellow-edged fins, and blue stripes on its face. Triggerfish are beautiful and fascinating to watch.

lei triggerfish

207

pinktail triggerfish

scrawled filefish

spotted surgeonfish

goldring surgeonfish

FILEFISH

The scrawled filefish has blue scribbles and brown dots over its olive green body. Quite large, up to one meter, often in pairs, but seen occasionally in groups.

A filefish will often turn its body flat to your view, and raise its top spine in order to impress you. This lets you have a great close-up view—and a perfect photo opportunity.

SURGEONFISH

Razor-sharp fin-like spines on each side of the tail are the hallmark of this fish, quite common in Hawai'i. These spines provide excellent defense, but aren't needed to fend off tourists since surgeonfish can easily swim away.

Varieties includes the orangeband surgeonfish (with distinctive long, bright orange marks on the side), as well as the pretty blue Achilles tang, which has large bright orange spots surrounding the spines near the orange tail. The common yellow tang is completely yellow and smaller. The sailfin tang has dramatic vertical markings. It's less common, but easy to identify.

208

WRASSES

Wrasses are amazingly bright and multicolored fish. Hawai'ian cleaner wrasses set themselves up for business and operate cleaning stations, where they clean much larger fish without having to worry about becoming dinner. They eat parasites, and provide an improbable reef service in the process. Perhaps their bright colors serve as neon signs to advertise their services. Hang out near their cleaning stations for excellent fish viewing. In Hawai'i, the tiny cleaner wrasse (about two inches) is neon yellow, purple-blue and black.

Other wrasses are larger including the dazzling yellowtail (up to 15 inches), which is covered with glowing blue spots, many stripes, and a bright yellow tail. The juvenile yellowtail is bright orange with a few big white spots, looking completely different from the adult version.

The common saddle wrasse is endemic to Hawai'i. It is bright blue, with green, orange and white markings. Wrasses are common and related to parrotfish, but usually smaller.

eyestripe surgeonfish

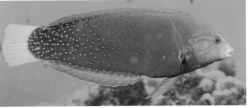
yellowtail coris

saddle wrasse

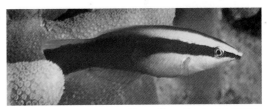
Hawai'ian cleaner wrasse

male bird wrasse

SCORPIONFISH

Hawai'ian lionfish

The Hawai'ian lionfish (sometimes called a turkeyfish) is very colorful example, with feather-like multicolored spines. Beware of their poisonous spines, though! Don't even think about touching a scorpionfish, and try to avoid accidentally stepping on one.

Other scorpionfish are so well-camouflaged that they are hard to see. They just lurk on the bottom blending in well with the sand and coral. If you see one, count yourself lucky, but don't step on it!

PUFFERFISH

male spotted toby

Pufferfish (and the related trunkfish) swim slowly due to their boxy shape, so need more protection. Puffers can blow up like prickly balloons when threatened.

Two kinds are common in sheltered areas: porcupine (displaying spines when inflated), and spotted trunkfish, boxfish and tobies (often brown or black with lots of white dots). Most tend to prefer to escape under the coral, although some seem unafraid of snorkelers and even curious. You may spot a big porcupine face peering out from under coral (giving the appearance of a much larger fish such as a shark).

The small spotted toby is common over the reef. The female is

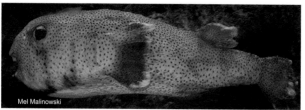

brown with white spots and the male is a beautiful dark blue with orange spots.

210

porcupinefish

SHARKS

Although sharks have quite a reputation for teeth rather than brains, they are unquestionably survivors, having been around for about 300 million years.

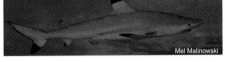

This is an extremely successful species with keen hearing, smell, sight and ability to detect electrical signals through the

blacktip reefshark

water. They swim with a side-to-side motion, which does not make them speedy by ocean standards.

When snorkeling you are unlikely to spot any shark except the whitetip or blacktip hanging around shallow water. Plenty of larger species pass by Hawai'i, but tend to travel the deeper waters further out in the channels.

DOLPHINS

Spinner dolphins are frequently seen in large schools (at least 200). They swim as small family groups within these schools, and often swim fast, leaping out of the water to spin in the air. They tend to hang out in certain locations, so you can search for them if you like.

spinner dolphin

spinner dolphins

Spinners are a bit sleeker than other dolphins and arrive at large bays to rest during the day. Dolphins sleep on one side at a time, so they can swim while resting.

211

Bottlenose dolphins often approach fast-moving boats, and it is a great thrill to watch them race along just in front of the bow of your boat, jumping in and out of the water with grace and easy speed.

Beaked and spotted dolphins are also commonly seen in the waters off Hawai'i.

bottlenose dolphins

SEA TURTLES

Green sea turtles (the most common in Hawai'i) are becoming more plentiful lately and seem to be less concerned about snorkelers.

Sea turtles are often seen in pairs. Larger specimens (often seen along the southwest shore) can be up to 100 years old, and tend to be docile and unafraid. You'll often see them resting on the bottom in about ten to twenty feet of water during the day. They sometimes let you swim as close as you like, but it's best to avoid hovering over them because they do need to come up for air. Just before dusk, they often hunt for algae along the lava coastline and don't seem to mind being tumbled against the sharp rocky shore.

Do not disturb these graceful creatures, so they can remain unafraid to swim among snorkelers. In Hawai'i it is against the law to touch or harass sea turtles. Enjoy, but don't crowd them.

green sea turtle

WHALES

Humpback whales migrate here to breed in winter, around December through early April. Humpbacks come quite close to the coast, and are most numerous in February. They are so large that you can often easily see them spouting and breaching. Their great size never fails to impress, as does their fluid, seemingly effortless graceful movement in the water. Many excursions offer whale-watching trips during the winter season. Listen for the whales when you snorkel.

humpback whales

Weather

All islands have a windward side, which is wetter, and a leeward side which is drier. In Hawai'i, the northeast is windward and hence wet, and the southwest is leeward, or kona, and hence drier and sunnier. Waves from afar tend to arrive from the north in winter and from the south in summer, although big swell can arrive from any direction at just about any time of year.

Hawai'i gets most of its rain in the winter. The most severe storms (called kona) come from the south and can even bring hurricanes in the summer. Temperatures tend to be very mild year-round, yet there is huge variety around the Big Island on any day of the year. There are days when you could tan in Kailua in the morning, drive up to cold Mauna Kea later, while warm rain continues in Hilo. Summer temperatures are five to eight degrees F warmer than winter.

Evaporating moisture from the ocean forms clouds. As the clouds rise over the mountains, they cool, and the condensing moisture becomes rain. Hilo receives about 180 inches of rain a year, while Kawaihae only gets about 5 inches, and the dry areas around Ka'u receive even less.

Having lost most of their moisture in passing over the mountains, the clouds have little left for the leeward side—so it is in the rain shadow of the mountains. The leeward weather is therefore often sunny. Waikīkī, Po'ipū, Kā'anapali, and Kailua are in rain shadows. On Hawai'i, if you get stuck with heavy rains in Hilo, just head for South Kohala, and you're very likely to find the sun.

Changeable is the word for Hawai'i's weather—not just between areas, but also rapidly changeable in any given place. The trade winds blow about 90% of the time in the summer and about 50% in the winter. They tend to be stronger in the afternoon and are stronger in South Kohala where air is funneled between the mountains.

The windward or northeastern coasts have much more rain, wind and waves—something important to remember when snorkeling. The most dependable and pleasant snorkeling in Hawai'i is on the Kona side. Yet, there are occasional times during the year when calm conditions on the windward side allow access to enjoyable snorkeling areas there. If the odds of good conditions are just too small, we don't review these areas.

Seasonal Changes

Hawai'i has much milder weather than the continental United States, yet it is has seasons you might call winter, spring and summer. At

20°N Latitude, there are nearly 2 1/2 hours more sun in midsummer than in midwinter, which is 21% more. But the moderating effect of the ocean keeps temperature swings quite moderate.

Winter is the cooler, wetter season. Cooler is a relative term, as the average high temperature in winter falls to a brisk 80° F, as opposed to a summer average high of 86° F. Low temperatures in Hawai'i may dip as low as 60 degrees, but more commonly are not below the high 60s even in winter.

Water temperature in winter falls to around 75° F, and at times, wind, rain and cooler air temperatures can temper your desire to splash around in the water. Winter usually begins in mid-November, with the start of winter storms from the north-northwest. This is the start of the large wave season on the north coast. Winter tails off in mid-March.

Spring really is just the transition from winter to summer, and is marked by the end of winter storms in mid-March. Hours of sunshine go up, especially on the west, leeward side of the island. This can be a very pleasant time of year. Spring transitions into summer in May.

Summer begins in May, as the weather warms, and the rains slacken. Trade winds temper the heat and humidity almost all the time. This is prime sunning and play time. An occasional tropical storm or hurricane can come through, and swell can roll in from the south. The heat softens in October as summer draws to an end.

Water Temperature

On the surface, the water in Hawai'i gets as low as 75° F in March to as high as 80° F (27° C) in September. Sheltered bays can be a bit warmer, while deeper or rough water can be surprisingly cool. Kaua'i, being furthest north of the main islands, is typically a little cooler than the other main islands. If you happen to be slender, no longer young, or from a moderate climate, this can seem cooler than you might like—especially if you like to snorkel for hours.

Hurricane

Summer is possible hurricane season, but it is also the time when weather is typically excellent. While the storms don't last long, they can be terribly destructive. Hurricanes can bring amazingly heavy rain and winds to the islands. Any could receive a direct hit, which happened when Hurricanes 'Iwa (1982) and later much stronger 'Iniki (see page 87) clobbered Kaua'i. Fortunately very few hurricanes ever actually hit Hawai'i directly.

Month by Month

JANUARY   This month offers an opportunity for the wettest weather all year. It's also one of the coolest. Large surf can often pound the north and west exposed beaches of Hawai'i.

FEBRUARY   Just as cool, the surf continues to hit the north and west exposed beaches, although storms are a bit less frequent than January. Occasionally, there will be a week when the wind and swell drop, the visibility clears, and snorkeling and diving conditions are superb. There is no way to predict when this will occur, however.

MARCH   The weather starts to improve with fewer storms, especially in the west.

APRIL   Spring arrives early, so warm weather begins during this month. Expect a few late swells, but also more calm, beautiful periods.

MAY   Summer is already arriving—especially in the south and west. This tends to be a trouble-free month. Mid to late May is one of our favorite snorkeling times, and few tourists are around, so you can feel like you have beaches to yourself.

JUNE   This offers very warm and dry weather with plenty of sun. Fortunately the winds blow nearly every day. Early June is usually great snorkeling weather, and the crowds have not arrived.

JULY   Much the same as June, except that storms in the South Pacific begin at this time. They hit beaches exposed to the south (called south swell).

AUGUST   Another warm month, occasional big waves can hit the southern exposed beaches (more south swell).

SEPTEMBER This end of summer can sometimes be the hottest and most humid. Hurricanes can strike Hawai'i, and are most common this month. Most will miss the islands, but bring muggy weather. 'Iniki, however, brought widespread damage to Kaua'i. The Big Island has seldom been seriously affected. This can be a great month in the water.

OCTOBER   Milder weather begins this month with the start of storms arriving from the north.

NOVEMBER   The first real winter storms arrive this month, and they can be somewhat cool. Since they stir up the water, visibility usually goes down.

DECEMBER   This is winter with frequent storms and wind bringing big waves to the exposed northern and western beaches. However, even this month can be clear and warm between storms.

Coolest month:	February
Hottest month:	September
Rainiest month:	January
Driest month:	June
Coolest water:	December-April
Warmest water:	August-September

Tsunami

Huge waves can be triggered by earthquakes either in the islands or far across the Pacific. Though quite rare, separated by decades usually, they've hit Hawai'i a number of times, more often from the northeast. Depending on the exact direction, they can directly hit a valley and really wipe it out and rinse it clean. It is better to not be there when this happens. Groups of tsunami waves are spaced about fifteen to twenty minutes apart, and often catch unsuspecting folks who go down to the beach too soon.

There's likely to be plenty of warning due to ever-vigilant earthquake monitoring equipment, elaborate modeling systems, and large numbers of beach-side tsunami warning sirens. Authorities prefer to warn of every possible tsunami just to be safe. It doesn't pay to ignore warnings just because the sea appears calm. If a major earthquake strikes while you're visiting, it's a good idea to head rapidly for high ground. Leave bays or valleys which can act to funnel the effects of a large wave.

Due the superior forecasting and warning systems now in place, Hawai'i is unlikely to ever experience the extreme but not forewarned destruction of the huge Indonesian tsunami of December 26, 2004. To help insure that this is so, when you hear a loud warning siren, without a good reason to know it is just a test, play it safe and leave the beach immediately for high ground.

Language

English is now the official language of the islands of Hawai'i (except for the island of Ni'ihau.) However, most place names and lots of slang come from Hawai'ian, so it's helpful to at least be able to pronounce enough to be understood. It's a very straight-forward phonetic language: each letter is usually pronounced just one way. The long place names aren't nearly so daunting when you have learned the system.

All syllables end with a vowel. When the missionaries attempted to write this oral language, they used only seven consonants (h,k,l,m,n,p,w). However, there is actually an eighth consonant in spoken Hawai'ian, the glottal stop (called an 'okina)—marked by the '. This is not the same as an apostrophe: '. When you say 'Uh-oh' in American English, you are using a glottal stop.

Five vowels (a,e,i,o,u) were used by the missionaries, but there are actually five more, the same vowels pronounced with a longer glide and more stress: ā, ē, ī, ō, and ū. A horizontal line (called a kahakō) is placed over these vowels. Nēnē, for example, is pronounced like "Nehh-Nehh" with a little 'a' in there, soft. We have attempted to include all kahakōs (macrons) and 'okinas, so it will be easier for our readers to pronounce the words properly. Researching proper place names is a challenge, as some of the proper spellings and meanings are being lost. If we have made mistakes, we hope our more knowledgeable Hawai'ian readers will understand and let us know for future editions.

Each and every letter is pronounced in Hawai'ian, except for a few vowel combinations. However, locals often shorten names a bit, so listen carefully to the way natives pronounce a name.

Another addition to the language is a form of pidgin, which served to ease the difficulties of having multiple languages spoken. Laborers were brought in speaking Japanese, Mandarin, Cantonese, Portuguese, English, as well as other languages, and they had to be able to work together. Pidgin evolved as an improvised, but surprisingly effective way to communicate, and much of it survives in slang and common usage today. It's very interesting to hear and learn, but we'd suggest you be very circumspect about using it unless you study it carefully. It can sound affected from the mouth of a tourist, possibly coming off as if you're mimicing and disrespecting locals. It may be better to just listen and enjoy the lilt.

Pronunciation

Consonants are pronounced the same as in English, except that the W sounds more like a V when it appears in the middle of a word.

Unstressed vowels are pronounced as follows:

a = *a* in *a*bove
e = *e* in b*e*t
i = *y* in cit*y*
o = *o* in s*o*le (without off glide)
u = *oo* in m*oo*n (without off glide)

Stressed vowels are a little different, and none have off glides:

a or ā = *a* in f*a*r
e = *e* in b*e*t
ē = between 'ehh' and *ay* in p*ay* *(not quite that hard)*
i or ī = *ee* in s*ee*
o or ō = *o* in s*o*le
u or ū = *oo* in m*oo*n

When pairs of vowels are joined (as they often are), pronounce each, with slightly more emphasis on the first one. This varies somewhat with local usage. It is beyond the scope of this book to teach the complexities of spoken Hawai'ian, but maybe we'll get you started.

Learning to respect and pronounce some Hawai'ian will bring you closer to the heart of the Hawai'ian culture. Our goal is to make you aware enough that you can understand what you are hearing, and not be daunted by the many beautiful, but multisyllabic words.

Kealakekua, for example, is not so hard: it has four syllables: Ke.ala. ke.kua and means: Ke (The) ala (pathway) (of) ke (the) kua (gods). Now you're ready for humuhumunukunukuāpua'a (the state fish of Hawai'i): humu.humu.nuku.nuku.āpu.a'a. See, it's easy once you divide it up!

After you get the hang of it, you may come to feel, as we have, that Hawai'ian is one of the most mellifluous languages on earth. This may be part of the reasons songs in Hawai'ian have become popular far beyond the islands. Modern folksingers such as Iz (Israel Kamakawiwa'ole) and Keali'i Reichel have contributed by writing and singing beautiful new songs in Hawai'ian. Listening to their new as well as traditional songs is a great way to learn the pronunciation of this delightful language!

Index

About the Authors

Judy and Mel Malinowski love to snorkel in the warm oceans of the tropics.

This love has led them to embark on snorkeling and cultural adventures to 70-some countries from Anguilla to Zanzibar. Hawai'i kept drawing them back, infusing their lives with aloha and teaching respect for the 'āina.

Although they are certified scuba divers, the lightness and freedom of snorkeling keeps it their favorite recreation. Whenever possible, they are in the ocean every morning by seven a.m.

Mel, Judy and their three children have hosted students and cultural exchange visitors from Bosnia, Brazil, China, Germany, Nepal, New Zealand, Serbia, and Turkey in their home, and helped hundreds of other families enrich their lives through cultural exchange.

Working with exchange students and traveling as much as their businesses allow has encouraged their interest in the study of languages from Mandarin Chinese to Hawai'ian. They are graduates of Stanford University.

Mel and Judy live on the South Kohala coast of the island of Hawai'i.